T0147556

Between Roxbury and a Hard Place

Place

Growing up during the Great Depression 1932 - 1943

by

Gerald Factor

iUniverse, Inc.
New York   Bloomington

Between Roxbury and a Hard Place
Growing Up During the Great Depression 1932 to 1943

iUniverse books may be ordered through booksellers or by contacting:

iUniverse
1663 Liberty Drive
Bloomington, IN 47403
www.iuniverse.com
1-800-Authors (1-800-288-4677)

Because of the dynamic nature of the Internet, any Web addresses or links contained in this book may have changed since publication and may no longer be valid. The views expressed in this work are solely those of the author and do not necessarily reflect the views of the publisher, and the publisher hereby disclaims any responsibility for them.

ISBN: 978-1-4401-2166-1 (pbk)
ISBN: 978-1-4401-2167-8 (ebk)

Printed in the United States of America

iUniverse rev. date: 03/26/2009

Contents

Acknowledgements

Fortune has smiled upon me for many years in the form of my Rancho Bernardo Writers Group. Every week I am happy to spend Friday mornings with them because they are so wonderful and helpful. We read and critique each other's writing, providing our best judgment and knowledge about our craft. We also help each other with marketing.

So, besides being in the company of great friends, I have the benefit of being with writing experts.

I am grateful for the support of each member of the group. They are: Peter Berkos (our leader), Karl Bell, Robert Fertig, Lillian Herzberg, Aaron Hock (deceased), Diana Kahn, Rosalie Kramer (she suggested the title), Don McGee, and Lori Nails-Smoote.

Credit for the cover photo goes to Allan and Terry Shechet, model and photographer respectively.

Glossary of Yiddish Terms

bubeleh - a diminutive term of endearment, such as sweety or little
    loved one.

challah or chale - egg bread (pronounced with the gutteral ch)

kholeria af ihm - a curse, literally a cholera on him

dovening - praying with a rhythmic bending movement of the
    upper body

Gerreleh – The diminutive affectionate form for Gerry

ihm - him

kinder - children

klutz - a clumsy person. Literally - a block of wood

nosh - snack

nosherie -foods for snacking

mitzvah - a good thing or a good deed , also a commandment.

motzi - the prayer said over the bread before eating,

putz - penis, derogatory when referring to a person.

schlemiel - bungler, misfit

schlep - drag

shiksa - a non-Jewish female

yeshiva bocher - students at the Jewish Seminary (literally: school
    boys)

voorsht - sausage, salami

Chapter 1

The Separation

1932

"Yes, he's gone. He left me all alone vid two little kids!" I remember my mother, Sonia Factor tearfully repeating the terrible words to her close friend Etty Goldman. "That *putz* ran off with a *shiksa*! *Oy a choleria af ihm!*" she said in Yiddish which I understood at the age of 7 but wished I didn't. (I didn't know what putz meant, but I knew it was supposed to be my father.) That my father had left us was not what I wanted to hear. My mother was obviously very upset when she calls the cholera curse on him. Then she continued through her tears, "How are ve going to ged along vidout him? How vill ve get money and food to live?"

"Sonia, Sonia," Etty said soothingly, "don't vorry bout dat. Your friends aren't going to let you and your kids starfe. If you esk me, I tink you are just as vell off vidout dat *schlemiel* , Norman. He alvays had an eye for de vimmin. And he never could hold a job because he is such a communist dat he calls every boss he ever had a greedy kepitalist. Who vants to listen to dat? So dey fire him."

"I knew about his affairs but I tot he'd outgrow dem and settle down and be a good husbin and fadder - but I vas wrong!" She was barely understandable as her voice squeaked through her tears.

I was hearing this through the partially open door of my bedroom which was across the hall from the living room where my mother and Mrs. Goldman were. I was on the verge of tears too as was usually the case when my mother cried - which had been too often during the past few years. She always sought me out to hug me when she was unhappy.

* * *

That was the prelude to our moving to the Roxbury suburb of Boston from Haverhill, Massachusetts in 1932 - during the depths of the Great Depression. As far as getting money to live on, there was little difference whether he was around or not. As Mrs. Goldman said, he had been completely unsuccessful in holding a job. He also failed at running any little business enterprise he started. His businesses could not employ any person other than himself because otherwise he would become a capitalist - which was unforgivable in his eyes. He never made enough money to hire somebody so such ideas were completely meaningless at the time but that did not inhibit him from voicing his opinions on the subject.

He was also a failure in maintaining a civil relationship with his wife because I remember how they squabbled all the time. It seemed to me they were always yelling at each other, often about me. "Gerry eat your dinner!" was a refrain from both of them I'll never forget. I was told that arguments involving me started when I was born. My father's atheism prompted him to refuse to have me circumcised and that he and my mother had a major row on that topic. My mother won that round - I have the evidence to prove it. As far back as I can remember they were always bickering if not about my eating, it was about what I was wearing or doing. So, although I didn't want them to split, I didn't cry when they did.

Their separation was inevitable because of their drastically different views on politics and about life in general as well as their intellectual attitudes. My father was a Trotskyite, and my mother was a plain ordinary unquestioning communist. Norman was very relaxed and laissez-faire about bringing up the children whereas Sonia wanted the kids to behave just so and to eat and behave properly according to her rules. Even though they both immigrated to the United States from Russia at about the same time with no knowledge of English, my father grasped the language very quickly and spoke fluently without an accent in just a few years, whereas my mother spoke her sparse English with a heavy accent and used Yiddish most of the time.

They may have also hollered at each other about my sister, Ruth, but I don't remember any of that. She was six years older than I.

Sonia Factor got a job sewing piecework in one of the shoe factories in Haverhill but she did not bring home enough money to support her little family of three. Her brother-in-law, my Uncle Frank, who was a foreman in a different shoe factory, had to augment her income every week for us to make ends meet. He was the husband of my mother's sister Sarah who had died three years earlier. He was wonderful to us, and by virtue of his having been in the country at least two years longer than we, he was able to show us the ropes. He was a big man with a strong, deep voice that inspired respect. His English was very good, although he still occasionally lapsed into an accent. This situation with him laying out money for us every week clearly could not continue indefinitely.

"Sonia, like we discussed last week, I have made arrangements for you and Ruthie and Gerry to move to Roxbury." Uncle Frank's manner was very gentle and sympathetic, but at the same time it was clear that this was not a subject for discussion. This was how it had to be. My mother normally accepted everything Uncle Frank said without question since it was he who made it possible for her to come to the U.S. from Liten, a little town near Kiev in Russia.

"You'll move right in with the Greenbaums. Reuven Greenbaum has a partner and together they own the G&B Delicatessen on Dudley Street, so you know right away that there will be no trouble getting food, and the same thing with money. They'll be able to take care of you until you find someone to live with for good. And they have a daughter about the same age as Gerry, so he'll have someone to play with.

"Frenk, vat do you mean, somevun to live vid for good?"

"Ima and Reuven know a lot of people, and there are several families where they live who have broken up for different reasons. They'll introduce you around and maybe you'll find somebody you like and who likes you and you will be able to make a life together."

"Who vood vant me vid two little kids?" Sonia asked through trembling lips.

"Don't worry about that for two reasons. First, you are still a good-looking lady and second, some of the single men have children too. So - you may end up with a little bigger family than you have now, but at least you'll have a roof over your head and food in your stomach."

Sonia nodded thoughtfully as she accepted Frank's plan.

Chapter 2

The Move to Roxbury

Moving in with the Greenbaums was a simple matter. We arrived at #6 Howland Street carrying our satchels with all our clothing. The remainder of our worldly goods was being held for us in Haverhill at the homes of friends. On that Sunday morning in October 1932, we were greeted by Ima and Reuven with hugs and kisses and understanding murmurings about our situation and how happy they were to be able to help us. Ima's black hair with the few streaks of grey made her look a lot older than my mother with her red hair, although they were about the same age I learned later.

"Come Sonia and *kinder*," Ima said looking at Ruthie and me and pointing toward the kitchen, "Ve'll have some tea and cookies." I made a slight face at the mention of tea tht Ima noted. "If you vant, you can have hot chocolate," she continued. She was pleased by my smile. We put our bags down in the hallway and went to the already set table. After we finished our refreshments Ima said, "Come, I'll show you vhere you'll sleep." We went into the den that was a small doorless room between their bedroom and the dining room.

"Sonia, you'll sleep on de sofa; Ruti, you can sleep on de easy chair with de foot rest in front, and Gerry you'll sleep on blankets on de floor." We were aghast at the arrangement, but managed to hide our feelings because we realized how much trouble the Greenbaums were going through to fit us into their small flat.

What we did not know, was that the Greenbaums had a strong motivation to take care of us, a motivation that went well beyond just friendship. Ima had a brother, Sol Samuels, who's wife had been in a mental hospital for many years, and he had four children who had been living in a Jewish orphan home, and were now living in foster homes. Sol was looking for someone with whom to live to enable him to bring his family together. Reuven and Frank were plotting together to see if they could arrange a *shidach* - an arranged marriage of the two families.

Our arrangement at the Greenbaums house was bad to say the least, but it was definitely better than nothing and we knew that it was not going to last long this way. As a matter of fact, it lasted less than a week. Rueven found a third floor apartment for us three blocks away on Gaston Street. He and Uncle Joe were sharing the expense until we could become self-sufficient. Every time Uncle Joe came to visit from Haverhill he brought with him some of the items we were storing with our friends.

Our apartment on Gaston Street was a barren affair even when eventually we had acquired all our belongings from Haverhill. We were fortunate that Uncle Joe was able to own an automobile on his foreman's salary at the shoe factory. That was how he was able to bring us all of our boxes and small pieces of furniture. He was able to borrow a small truck to deliver us our beds and our one dresser.

It was a three-bedroom apartment and all of our stuff hardly made a dent towards filling it up. There were no carpets on the floors, the windows had ragged pull down blinds, several of the lights were just bare bulbs. But it was home to us, and for that reason we liked it.

Chapter 3

You Show Me Yours and I'll Show You Mine.

The William Lloyd Garrison grammar school was about a mile and a half away. I knew how to go because the Greenbaum's daughter, Rachel, had taken me to register for the first time during the week that we had lived with them. She was just a few months older than I, but we did not end up in the same class. School was already in session when we arrived in Roxbury and the first thing I had to do was to take a test to see if the third grade was right for me. Apparently they liked what I did because they put me in a rapid advancement class - we did three grades in two years. It was nice, because the entire class stayed together through to the sixth grade.

One evening my mother said, "Come, Gerreleh, ve go to de Greenbaums for supper tonight. Rutie has to stay home to do homevork." So we walked the three blocks to their house. After supper the talk turned to playing whist, but there were only three adults who knew how to play and they needed a fourth.

"Goldie next door plays," Ima said, " and her husband likes to listen to de radio or read in de evening, so let me call her and see if ve can go over dere to play. I'll give her a call and see if dey fil like it."

When they left, Rachel and I were sitting at the kitchen table, the parents had left us a deck of cards and Sophie said, "Vile ve're next door, you kids can play vohr."

As soon as the parents left, Rachel looked at me and exclaimed gleefully, " Great - we're alone- Gerry, let's play doctor! We don't have to play war."

I looked at her apprehensively and stammered, " I - I don't think I know how to play doctor. Don't we need one of those things they listen with - it begins with an es."

"We can make believe we have a stethoscope. It'll all be make believe," Rachel exuberantly said.

"I've only seen a doctor once, a few years ago when I had a sore throat. All she did was stick a stick in my mouth and told me to say ah. What's so much fun about that?"

"You're right, that's not the fun part. The fun part is when we take off our clothes."

"TAKE OFF OUR CLOTHES! You're kidding aren't you?"

"No I'm not kidding."

"The only time I get naked is in the bath tub and the only one who can see me is my mother."

"See! See! That's the whole problem right there! Nobody can see you but your mother! They keep it a big secret and we never get to see it. Don't you ever wonder how a girl is different from a boy? I bet you don't even know that girls don't have a peeni. Do you? Have you ever seen a girl without clothes?"

"I once saw a statue of a naked lady in a museum," I volunteered. "But you're right, there was nothing between her legs."

"Wouldn't you like to see what I have between my legs?" Rachel whispered.

I stared at her for a long time before I nodded slowly. Then she said, "I'll show you mine if you'll show me yours. I've never seen a boy's thing." Again my response was a long time in coming, and when I nodded slowly I was looking at her sideways from the corners of my eyes. Rachel had been waiting for that nod, and as soon as she saw it she jumped up from her chair and standing in front of me, she reached under her skirt and pulled her bloomers down, stepped out of them and kicked them onto a chair.

"OK, Gerry, now you drop you pants, then when you take off your underpants I'll pick up my skirt, all right?"

"I don't have underpants, I have a union suit. It is all one piece."

"That's OK, it has buttons in front, right? You can open it all the way down and I'll be able to see your thing. Then you can drop the back so I can see your behind too."

I thought that it was all very interesting and I loved the idea of learning what all the mystery was about but I still felt a little uncomfortable. After my pants were off, I slowly unbuttoned the union suit until my little penis was sticking out. While I did that, Rachel lifted her skirt. We both stood quietly staring at each other's mini-organs.

I could see that Rachel was having the same reaction that I was having - which could best be characterized by - interesting but what's the big deal? Then I decided to take the initiative that so far had been all hers. "Turn around so I can see your behind." Which she did.

"That part looks just like mine. I once looked at mine in a mirror." Then I turned around, unbuttoned the drop seat of the union suit for her. She looked for a moment.

"No more secret. Come on, let's play war," Rachel said as she pulled her bloomers back on and picked up the cards.

When our parents returned, they commented, "It's good dat Gerry and Rachel play togedder so nice."

Chapter 4

My First Job

"Hello Mr. Weiner, remember me? You always give me a piece of candy when I come shopping with my mother."

"Of course I remember you, Gerry. What can I do for you today? You want another piece of candy?" he said with a broad smile. He owned the grocery store on the corner of Gaston and Warren Streets.

"No, no. Do you think - - do you think - - could I deliver some orders for you for money? I'll do them for five cents apiece." Mr. Weiner took lots of orders by telephone and many customers didn't want to carry their bags home; so he always had bags lined up on the floor marked with the names and addresses where they were supposed to be delivered. He usually closed the store at five o'clock in the afternoon, and then he loaded up his wheelbarrow-like pushcart and went around the neighborhood delivering all the orders.

Mr. Weiner gave me a skeptical look and said, "Gerry, you know how heavy some of these bags can be, and you know that many of them have to go up to third floors. Do you really think you can handle them? You're not a very big boy."

"Oh Mr. Weiner, I'm sure I can do it. Really! Look!" and I went into the standard body builder pose to show off my biceps. I wasn't very tall, but I was strong. With a big smile Mr. Weiner gave me a hug. It was obvious that he liked me.

"Gerry, tomorrow come by after school and we'll see how it goes."

On the first day of my new job, Mr. Weiner gave me two bags and sent me to two nearby addresses. By the time I got to the first one, my arms ached fiercely but I managed to ignore them until I climbed the stairs to the third floor and put down the bags. "Who's there?" came the reply to my knock. "It's Gerry with your order from Weiner's" The door opened and I was invited in and told to put the order on the kitchen table. Then she handed me a dime and said with a big smile, "Thank you very much." I smiled back and answered with "Thank YOU!" The same thing happened when I delivered the second order, although there, the tip was only a nickel. On the following day, I accompanied Mr. Weiner with his big pushcart filled with bags and helped him carry the orders up to the various customers, and I was thrilled to be collecting not only a nickel a bag from Mr. Weiner but many tips from the customers too. After a while, I went with the pushcart by myself. Sometimes I made more that $3.00 in a week that I gave to my mother.

* * *

"Look at dis!" My mother appeared ludicrous waving a long salami in the air. "Vere did dis *voorsht* come from? Anybuddy know? It vasn't here ven I left." It was a mystery - neither Ruth nor I could shed any light on the subject. This little mystery was solved fourteen years later when my father told me how he had come to Gaston Street hoping to see his children playing near the house. Failing that, he had gone up to the apartment - the door was never locked - and looked into the icebox. He panicked when he saw that there was no food in it. He ran to Weiner's grocery, bought the salami, ran back and put it in the icebox for his estranged family to have something to eat. His friend Reuven had told him where we were.

Chapter 5

Connecting with the Samuels Family

"Ve are moving next Saturday," my mother announced at dinner very casually as though it was a perfectly normal thing to be happening. "Ve are moving in vid de Samuels family. I'll be de house keeper, and ve'll all live togedder, de tree of us and de five of dem. Mr. Samuels, Sol, is a stitcher in a shoe fectry in Boston and brings home a reglar veeks pay. He is Ima Greenbaum's a brudder. He has tree boys and vun goil. Dey are all older den you. De mudder is sick and alvays in a hospital for a long time. De eight of us vill move to de toid floor of 18 Georgia Street in a four bedroom apartment."

Later when I was alone with Ruthie, I said, "Eight of us in four bedrooms doesn't sound great. We all will have a roommate. I hope they are nice. What do you think?"

"Gerry," she said, "we'll have to make it work, because we need them and they need us. Don't worry about it."

* * *

On Saturday morning Sol Samuels and his youngest son, David, showed up at our house on Gaston Street. My mother introduced us and then pointed at a suitcase for each of us to carry; Sol and Dave each carried two. We stopped several times to rest as we walked the seven blocks on Warren Street to where Blue Hill Avenue joined it at the spacious square called Grove Hall. There we turned right on Georgia Street and crossed over to number 18 on the corner of Segel Street.

"Hey Ma, you said we'd live on the third floor - this is the FOURTH floor! You didn't count the stairs from the street up to the first floor porch.!"

"Yeah, Ruthie's right." I said breathlessly, as I struggled to drag my suitcase up to the top floor.

"Gerry, you go into dat room at de end of the hall." Ma pointed to the right when we came in the front door. "Rutti, you go into dat room dere," she pointed at the door just to the left and across the hall from the front door. "You both have de bottom draws of de dressers in de rooms. Rutti take the bed near de door, Sally vill have de vun near de vindow. Gerry you take de bed on the left and Davie vill have de vun on de right near de vindow."

Dave was the only one home, Sally, Larry and Albert were all working - which was remarkable for a family during the depression. Eighteen-year-old David also had a job, but he was off on this Saturday. Here was a family of five and every one of them had a job - wow! But all of their wages together were barely enough to pay the rent for this big apartment and feed and clothe the eight of us.

"Ma, if I get job, will I still have to give you all my money?"

"I'll still need your money, because I don't get from Sol, except vot ve need for food, and dat is not much. But you can have an allowance of fifteen cents a veek."

I now lived too far from Mr. Weiner's grocery store to continue delivering orders so I figured that I'd have to find another job. I thought that I shouldn't have too tough a time, because a kid like me gets paid so little compared with a regular man. But I didn't know where to look - yet.

* * *

"OK pipsqueak, see that dresser - visualize a line on the floor starting at the middle of the bottom drawer and then all the way across the room to the door. You're gonna keep all your stuff to the left of the line - right?"

I looked up at the six feet of David to see if he was kidding around with me. His thin lips and pointy nose and unsmiling face made him look very serious so I answered, "Right." Then I continued with, "Where can I put my jacket?" I was looking at the closet which was on the wall near the foot of his bed.

David replied, "You can hang that on the right end of the pole - but nothing else of yours goes in there. Your shoes go under your bed."

It took only a moment to empty my little soft satchel into the bottom drawer and shove the empty bag under my bed on the left side of the room as my mother had directed. I had no problem with shoes because I was wearing my sneakers and had no others. I was not happy with my roommate because he seemed so bossy and trying to make himself look like a big man. I sensed that immediately and he never did anything to change that first impression.

My mother had been setting up the kitchen with food and utensils that Sol had earlier brought over from wherever they had lived before, and also with some of the things that we had carried over from Gaston Street. Our bigger items from there would be brought over in a truck by a friend of Sol's at a later time we were told. After we had put away our things, she made sardine sandwiches for us. Just as we finished lunch, Sally and Larry came home and we were introduced. Mother immediately and cheerfully made more sandwiches.

Sally was a good-looking twenty year old about 5.7" tall. "Where did you get that gorgeous red hair?" I asked, genuinely impressed, but also trying to make points with the pretty lady. Even at the age of seven, I was interested in ladies.

She smiled and replied, "From my mother. Obviously not from my father." She had the same pointy nose as David but her lips were fuller. Sally worked as a salesgirl at Filene's in Boston. She had a very pleasant way about her. Pleasant, but she spoke very tentatively giving the appearance of being unsure of herself. This was in stark contrast to her roommate, my sister Ruthie who was also very good looking, but almost five feet tall. There was never anything about her to suggest a lack of self-confidence. She had a solid athletic body. At the time, Ruthie was 13 years old and already a budding artist. Her drawings and paintings were striking and everyone who saw them immediately gasped and raved about how wonderful they were. But her strong manner came from more than that admiration, because she also felt a strong responsibility to help mother by filling in for the "man of the house" since we hadn't had one for many months. Which also meant that she was very bossy towards me. With my mother and sister both telling me what to do and not do, and now David too, I knew I was the low man on the totem pole.

Larry, 22, was a slightly built young man who spoke quietly and who also seemed insecure. He was about 5'6" tall with a full head of brown hair. He was finishing his studies at night school to become a lawyer while working during the day as a bookkeeper in a shoe factory in Boston; not the same one where his father worked. He was very pleasant to Ruthie and me - but especially to Ruthie.

Larry shared the front bedroom with Albert, 24, who came home later. Al worked for a printer and was the only one in the Samuels family who seemed to be self-confident. He was about 5'11" tall and very good looking. When he came home, he told us that he wouldn't be having dinner with us because he was eating with his fiancee, Glenda - at her folks.

* * *

Later, Ruthie and I were alone with my mother, Ruthie asked, "Where were Sol's kids living before they came here?"

"Vell, it's like dis. For a long time, de mudder vas in de hospital," and then she whispered, "for crazy people". And she continued in her normal voice, "De kids hev been goink from friend's house to friend's house, and den to de place for orphans - dey hev been kicked around a lot. Dat is vy dey are how dey are."

* * *

Finding a job at 7 years of age was not easy, but I eventually was hired to deliver papers. My route was within four blocks of where I lived, but since it went all around, there were a lot of houses to be serviced. I became adept at folding the papers and tossing them to the doors.

While I was generally an honest kid, I found that the temptations placed before me by this job were too much to resist. Many of the homes had milk bottles delivered to the doors, and sometimes a bag of bread and rolls from the bakery too. First I figured that the lady of the house wouldn't notice that the bag of rolls contained only 12 instead of the baker's dozen of 13 - so I got into the habit of stealing one from a different house each time. After a while, I got tired of eating the dry rolls, and I occasionally stole a quart of milk from the houses that received more than four quarts every morning. I had no trouble drinking the whole quart of milk with a roll. I got away with that for more than a year without getting caught. Then I decided that I was tempting fate and I stopped stealing. Besides, I didn't feel good about it. That was the entire scope of my career in crime. I held that job for four years till I was 11. I don't remember why it stopped.

Chapter 6

The Bully

When I returned home after school I went down the back stairs onto Segel Street to see what was going on.

"Hey kid! What's your name?"

"Gerry, what's yours?" I replied as I warily looked over the speaker who appeared to be older than I and twice my size, mostly in width.

"I'm Manny. Wanna play?"

"What are you playing?"

"Stick ball," he said.

"What's that?"

Displaying a small rubber ball and a length of broomstick he said, "We fungo the ball down the street and then run two bases, one on each side of the street and then home. It's kinda like baseball." He tossed the ball up with one hand, and then whacked it with the broomstick to demonstrate how to fungo. "If the ball is caught without a bounce, the batter is out or if he is tagged off base he's out too. It's okay to catch the ball off the buildings for an out. We can play two or four on a side, and we are only three, we need one more."

"Sounds like fun. Sure, I'll play."

Manny selected the teams, putting me with Wayne as a team against himself and Jason. I noted immediately that Wayne was a slow, clumsy kid and that both Jason and Manny were athletic and well coordinated. Manny had clearly chosen the teams so that his side would win. I, however, was also athletic and once I saw how to fungo, I did it very well. When the first game was over, Wayne and I had won by a small margin. Great - was my first reaction, but when I saw that both Manny and Jason were scowling, I sensed that I had made a mistake.

After the game, Wayne told me, "Manny rules the neighborhood. He is kina like a king. He's always the one who decides what we'll play and who can play. He likes to be the boss - and he likes to win. His family is rich; they own camera stores."

The next day I went down to play after school and found that the four boys were already playing stickball. During a pause in the play, I asked Jason if I could replace one of the losers when this game was finished. Before Jason could reply, I realized that I had made another mistake and that I should have known better especially after what Wayne had told me about Manny.

"Why the hell you asking him? You ask ME! Y'understand?" Manny said as he came next to me and thrust his belly forward bumping me so that I stumbled backwards. He started poking me in the chest with a stiff finger and then he started punching me lightly and then he was hitting me harder. I was astonished and desperately raised my hands in front of my chest, which resulted in the blows arriving on my face instead. When I tried to block the blows to my head they came again at my chest and stomach until I fell down sobbing and saying, "I'm sorry, I should have asked you instead of Jason." When Manny was satisfied with me sobbing on the ground and the other boys appropriately laughing and admiring his technique, he stopped the pummeling and returned to the game. I jumped up and ran home as fast as I could crying all the way. I burst into the kitchen where my mother was preparing dinner, I sobbed, "Manny beat me up!"

"How many times hev I told you not to fight? See vot heppens ven you fight?"

I'm confused - I wasn't fighting - Manny was fighting.

The next day I found the group playing dodge ball, which was a game any number could play. Willing to let by-gones be by-gones, I asked Manny if I could play.

"Look who's here, the new fairy on the block, and he wants to play too. What do you think of that?" he sneered. Without further ceremony he waded right in to beat me into a sobbing mass of quivering flesh, and again I ran home crying to mother.

"Vy are you fightink? I kip tellink you not to fight!" She carried on with this classical Jewish mother refrain while she ministered gently to my bloody nose and shiner. I went to my bedroom to sulk. *I hate that Manny. Tomorrow I'll find new kids to play with. I'm not going to let him do that to me again..* The next day after school, I went down the front steps and turned left towards Hartwell Street to find some other playmates - but the boys there were teenagers.

As I walked back I was scared because Manny might beat me up again. *Maybe Manny will change his mind. Maybe he won't want to beat me up again. Maybe the other boys won't laugh at me. Maybe - maybe he will beat me up.* I shuddered. My fear grew as I found myself at the corner of Segel Street. I saw the boys playing further up the block and although I was trembling, I walked toward them. I was quivering from head to toe and I wondered whether they could see how frightened I was. They stopped playing and Manny once again came toward me, smiling derisively.

"So the little boy wants to play again." He moved face-to-face with me. When Manny poked me on the chest with his finger, it was as though he hit the release button on a heavily loaded spring. I became a blur of flailing fists, elbows, knees, and feet and for about one and a half minutes, Manny received a beating the likes of which he had never seen, or given or imagined. Towards the end of the fight, the other boys dragged me off Manny's chest for fear that his bloodied head might be fractured against the sidewalk from which it was bouncing with each blow. This time it was Manny who ran home screaming to his mother. I was still quivering from head to toe and tears of rage streamed down my face as I gathered myself together after the fight. I had not received a single blow other than that first poke. The other boys backed away from me as I glared angrily at them but his time they were not laughing at me. As I wobbled my way home I was grateful that the others could not see how my knees were shaking inside my baggy knickers.

* * *

"Ma, I had another fight with Manny, but this time I beat him up. He started it again." My mother tried not to smile and said, "I tot I told you not to fight."

That evening, after supper there was a pounding on the back door. When my mother opened the door, Manny's mother stormed into the kitchen without waiting to be asked in and started hollering at my Ma.

"I had to take my Manny to the hospital to get xrays and he looks terrible. Your Gerry did it and I'm going to sue you for every cent you've got! You'll hear from my lawyer!" she bellowed while wagging her finger and alternating her glares from me to my mother.

"Vait, vait, Mrs. Manny's Mudder, your Manny beat up my Gerry two times before. Dis vould hef been de toid time."

"Never mind the excuses you'll hear from my lawyer!"

"Vait don't get so excited - I can safe you de expense from a lawyer. Vait, I hef it right here. Every cent I own." She reached into her handbag and pulled out a little change purse which she unsnapped and inverted and two dimes, a nickel and three pennies fell out. "Here you take dem." When she saw the incredulous look on Manny's mother's face, she continued. "Yes, dat's right. Dat's all de money I hef. I only verk here. I'm de housekeeper. I don't hef no money. Safe de lawyer expense."

Manny's mother snorted and stormed out without taking the money.

* * *

Within minutes after the fight, the entire under-twelve population of the area knew that the new pint-sized kid had beaten the daylights out of the neighborhood bully and had gotten away without a scratch. Fortunately they didn't talk about the previous beatings! Manny recovered with minor permanent marks and I acquired immense respect and prestige in the neighborhood. My reputation was such that I was never challenged or had another fight during the entire seven years that I lived there.

Chapter 7

Josh

A few weeks later, I was walking up Cheney Street on the way to school when I noticed a big kid coming out of a house just as I was about to pass by. He saw me and started to walk alongside and said, "Hi, you're Gerry aren't you?" It was more of a statement than a question.

"Yes, I am, who are you?"

"My name's Josh Kagan. Josh is short for Joshua. I live on the third floor of the building you just saw me come out of."

"How'd you know my name?"

"I heard about the new kid who just moved in and beat up Manny the neighborhood bully. I saw you one day playing dodge ball on Segel Street and someone pointed you out."

I felt a mixture of pride and fear with his comment; pride because my reputation was getting around; fear because Josh was at least 5'6" tall and I was barely 4 feet. Josh clearly was going to be a big guy when he grows up, I thought. Not only that, Josh was not a skinny kid like me, - he was real chunky. I wondered how old he was - definitely older than I. I was afraid he might want to challenge me to a fight to establish his supremacy in the neighborhood. I had heard that happened fairly often. I didn't need to worry about Josh though, because I found him to be a very pleasant, easy going, intellectual kid who would avoid hurting a fly. He normally never spoke badly about anyone – but on that day he said, "It was about time someone knocked him off his high horse. Between his money and his big belly he figures he can always have things go his way. What a spoiled brat he is. I understand he's changed thanks to you." I tried hard not to appear as though I was swelling with pride – which I was.

"What grade're you in?" Josh asked.

"I'm in the 4th – RA."

"What's RA?"

"Rapid Advancement, we take the 3rd and 4th grade together in one year and then the next year we go into the 5th. How 'bout you?"

"I'm in the 5th grade."

Josh and I took an immediate liking to each other.

Then Josh said, "How about coming over to my house after school and we can play some cards. What games do you know?"

"I can play Go Fish, War, and my mother taught me how to play Casino too."

"Great, come by at about quarter of four, we can play till 4:30 and then we'll listen to Jack Armstrong The All-American Boy, Buck Rogers, and Flash Gordon – ok?"

"Great, I never miss the serials."

"I never miss them either," Josh said.

"I can't wait to hear how Flash Gordon gets out of his latest pickle. The bad guys have him trapped and there's no way in the world he can get out."

"Don't worry, you'll see, they'll get him out in the nick of time, and he'll end up on top! That's the way of the serials. Every escapade leaves you holding your breathe for the hero and then the next chapter tells us about the things we didn't know that let him survive his impossible situations."

"You know, I think you're right! I never noticed that. I guess that's your advantage. How old are you?"

"I'm almost ten. How old are you?"

I hesitated because I feared that Josh might not want to be friends with a kid who was almost two years younger than he. "I'm eight," I said and immediately continued with, "You've been listening to the serials longer than I have and you've figured out their tricks."

"Right," he replied.

We talked about the radio serials and the Saturday movie serials too all the way to school "I like talking with you," he said, "The other kids are so damn dumb." There we separated to go to our different classes. Since we finished at different times, we didn't walk home together. At his house, I rang the bell and when he buzzed the door I walked up to the 3rd floor where he was waiting for me.

"Ma, this is Gerry I told you about."

With a big smile she said, "Come right in and have some milk and cookies."

"Thank you," I said with an eager smile.

After we had our *nosh*, I asked, "Can I use your phone to call my Ma, so she'll know where I am?"

"Of course. It's on that little table."

As I took the earpiece off the hook and started dialing, I read their number because I knew that my mother would want it. "Hi Ma, I'm at the Kagen's on Cheney St. with my new friend Josh. We just had milk and cookies. Is it ok if I stay here till supper time?"

"OK, good. Yes, here is their phone number, JU3- 4921".

"Where do you live, Gerry?" Mrs. Kagen asked.

"On the corner of Georgia and Segel Streets."

"Which shul does you family belong to?"

I looked at her with a blank stare and didn't know how to answer.

"Don't you go to shul every Friday?"

I knew the answer to that question, "No, we don't go anywhere on Friday because my mother always makes us boiled chicken for supper on Friday, and matzo ball soup. too."

She had a puzzled look on her face but didn't ask any more questions at that time.

* * *

While Josh and I were playing casino I asked, "When does your father come home?"

"He owns a bar- restaurant, and three days a week, including today, he leaves the bar about five o'clock and walks home from Quincy street along Blue Hill Avenue to Grove Hall. He gets home about twenty to six. The rest of the week, he closes at midnight. On those days, he goes in later and lets his assistant manager open for him the next morning."

"He owns a bar? Is that where people buy booze?"

"They can buy drinks, but not bottles there. They can have a sandwich too. Bottles they buy at a liquor store."

"Oh," I said as my education accumulated another bit of information.

Later, when I met his father, I realized how it came to be that I liked Josh as much as I did, - he had two wonderful parents. Mr. Kagen's warm smile was not hidden by his round metal-framed glasses. He was not a big man – his 10 year-old son, Josh, was already almost as tall as he. I could see the similarity in their round faces.

I grew to love them and they loved me too. Josh and I became inseparable. About four months after we first became acquainted, I overheard Mr. and Mrs. Kagen talking about me and Josh. We were in their living room listening to the radio and they were in the kitchen with the door closed, and I switched my concentration to what they were saying while Josh stayed glued to the radio. I had to strain to hear because their voices were muffled.

I heard Mrs. Kagen say, "Louis, it's so nice that Josh has found a close friend like Gerry. I am amazed when I hear those two kids talk! They are so young, especially, Gerry, but they talk like grownups. The two of them. And the things they talk about! You'd think they were ten years older than they are. It's so nice that they get along like they do. But you know something, Gerry's never been to a synagogue, and I'd like to ask him to go with us next time, is that ok with you?"

"Sure," Mr. Kagen answered.

So I wasn't surprised when Mrs Kagen later asked, "Gerry, How would you like to go with us to Shabbas services at the Crawford Street shul?"

"OK," I replied. For years, I had heard philosophic discussions among my mother's "intellectual" friends about God and religion, and how they argued back and forth. And I heard mentioned several times, "The religious Jews don't have to worry about the basics, they only worry about the interpretations and hows in the Talmud. The answers about God are given to them, and they are happy to accept them and not worry."

So when Mrs. Kagen asked whether I would like to go Sabbath services, I was willing and interested in learning about Judaism. Maybe then I wouldn't have to worry about whether or not there was a God. When Saturday morning came, I went early to the Kagens and walked the four blocks with them to the synagogue. I was impressed with the intensity I observed in the men with the prayer shawls on their shoulders and their rocking back and forth as they prayed. "That's called davening," Josh explained to me. I tried to pay attention to what was being said, but it was all in Hebrew.

"Josh, do you understand what they're saying?" I whispered.

"No I don't, but you can follow it along in this book. It's in Hebrew on the left, and in English on the right. We're on page 246 and notice that 247 is on the left not on the right. It's a different section every week. Next year, they start all over again."

"It's all about God. I thought it was going to be about life and people."

"That's just this section."

I was bored, bored, bored and I was relieved when the service finally ended. On another occasion, they invited me to a Friday night service, which I also failed to find interesting. But I liked this one much better because when it was over, everyone went into another room where there was *challah*, cookies and Manishewitz sweet cherry wine which I was not permitted to drink. They had punch for the kids. The Rabbi did a short ceremony over the *challah* that Josh explained to me was called a *motzi*. Two weeks later I accompanied them again and found that that section too was all about God – and I was again bored – and again I struggled to not fall asleep.

Much later, and after several more times I went with them to the Friday night services, the Kagens saw that I was not being motivated at all by what I was hearing. Mrs. Kagen said, "Gerry, if you would take the Sunday Hebrew classes with the Cantor, then you would understand what was being said, and it would be more interesting. If your parents don't want to pay for it, I think I could talk the Cantor into taking you for nothing, or at least for less, and my husband and I would be willing to pay for that."

I was touched by their offer and realized that they really wanted to help me become an observant Jew. They wouldn't make such an offer if they didn't like me a lot. But, I didn't believe what they were saying, because Josh had attended the Sunday school classes, and although he knew how to say the prayers in Hebrew, I knew that he didn't understand any of the other words.

"Thank you very much, Mrs. Kagen, I really appreciate your offer, but I don't want to do that. It's awfully nice of you. Maybe next year when I'm older."

* * *

Josh and I walked on Blue Hill Avenue towards Franklin Park and back hundreds of times during the ensuing six years, discussing such trivial subjects as astronomy, beginnings of life, religion, human behavior, sports, music, school, working, love, sex and girls.

During 1937, to take advantage of lower rent, we moved to Hansborough Street in Dorchester which was about two miles from Grove Hall. We only lived there for about one and a half years, after which we moved back to Roxbury for the same reason. Although we didn't live really close to each other any more, we still continued our walking. We'd meet somewhere and then walk to one home, and then we'd walk back to the other. Frequently, if our discussions hadn't reached a good breaking point, we'd then walk back again.

"Gerry, I honestly cannot understand how you still do not believe in God. How do you think all this came to be – by this, I mean everything," with spread arms.

"For my money, I think it all comes from nature and from man's brain."

"Yah, but what is nature and what is man?"

"Nature is what is all around us that is not made by man, and man is us – people."

"Right, now we're back to my question – how do you think this all came to be without God?"

My attention was momentarily distracted by my sweet tooth as we walked by a candy store next to the Franklin Park movie theatre. "Josh, I've got a nickel, let's stop in here and buy some candy."

"Sounds good to me!"

As we came out of the store, each of us munching on our half of a Baby Ruth, Josh continued with, "You were about to tell me how nature and man came to be without God, remember?"

"I didn't forget. It and we all evolved as in Darwin's theory."

"What the dickens is Darwin's theory – and where did you hear about it?"

"I was in the library one day and there were a coupla teenagers arguing loudly about something and the librarian came over and told them to be quiet or leave, and they left. The book they were looking at on the table was still open – it was from the encyclopedia. I was curious and went over and looked at the page they were arguing about. It was about Darwin's theory of evolution, and there was a simple chart listing the main things about it. His theory is that things change slowly over millions of years – living things especially, but I think it also applies to the mountains and rivers. Life started with one celled animals which grew to become us over millions of years."

"Bah! How can you talk about millions of years when the whole earth isn't that old?"

"The encyclopedia pointed out that fossils have been found that are millions of years old. Isn't that proof the earth is at least that old? The article also mentioned that the theory was very controversial because it says things that contradict what most religions say about the creation of the earth and life. By the way, I always thought it was kind of ridiculous to talk about the earth being created in six days and that Sunday was supposed to be a day of rest because God was tired."

Josh was a little indignant with that comment. "God wasn't tired. He said that because he didn't want US to get tired from working too hard. He was thinking about us." Then he continued, "Where did that one celled animal come from?"

"The book didn't mention that. I don't know. Maybe it came in on a spore on a meteor from space, or perhaps a lightening strike caused a change in something – I don't know but it had to start somewhere."

"Aha!" Josh exclaimed. "Yes, it had to start somewhere. Why couldn't that have been done by God?"

"It could have been IF you believe in God. But now you are talking about God creating a one-celled animal, not whole people! Why would he bother with one cell after he created the whole earth and the sky and Adam and Eve and everything else too?"

"He would bother because he knew how important life is!"

Now it was my turn. "Aha! So you accept the idea that people evolved from one-celled animals!"

"No, no Gerry, I do not accept that idea at all. I was just carrying on the argument. I still think that it was God who created people in the Garden of Eden. But - maybe it was a little longer ago than I originally thought - if the fossil evidence is really true."

"Well, I'm glad to see that you have at least a little doubt about the complete accuracy of what is written in the bible."

"Oh, I'm willing to do some interpreting. The *yeshiva bochers* are interpreting all the time. That's their whole aim in life!"

No matter how animated our discussions became, we were never angry at each other, - especially since we both knew our original positions; - exasperated – sometimes., angry - never,

Chapter 8

Segel Street Games

Segel Street was the center for afternoon playing when Josh and I were not walking. Besides stickball and dodge ball, we also played at cops and robbers and recreating our own dramatic versions of some of the radio serial episodes. We also played games on wheels – roller skates. We played a form of hockey, which helped us master our skating capabilities. I became very skilled and comfortable on roller skates. In addition to being a necessity for playing hockey, they became my primary mode of transportation.

When the games changed to skate scooters, I was distressed because I was unwilling the sacrifice my skates to make one. The skate scooter was a short piece of two-by-four with one half of a steel skate on each end which provided the foot rest and the wheels, and a two compartment orange crate for the upright part with handles for steering.

"No Josh, I won't used one of skates to make a scooter - I enjoy skating too much."

"But they look like so much fun. Manny and Wayne are both making one."

"Now, there's a thought! Each of them will be using one skate, so they should have a one left over they may be willing to sell cheap.

How about you going to Manny and offer him fifteen cents for his left over skate, and I'll do the same with Wayne?"

"Gerry! That's a great idea!"

Josh ended up paying twenty cents for his skate from Manny, and I paid twenty-three for mine from Wayne.

"A great investment to get us started!" Josh exclaimed. "OK, so now we have the wheels but where do you think we can get the wood and boxes we need?"

"I remember seeing some workers in Goldbman's Grocery. They were taking down a partition. I bet there's some scraps of wood in back of his store. Let's go look.."

We walked into the alley a short way towards the back of the grocery store. As we approached, we saw a big pile of plaster and splinters of wood.

"Gerry, look at this!"

Josh was holding up one corner of a slab of plaster exposing a long stud that was messed up on the ends but had a nice clean section in the middle.

"There's enough here for both of us if we can get it cut right." Gerry said. "Let's see if we can talk the handyman who is making this mess into cutting it for us. See if you can pull it out of the pile while I put on my helpless child look and try to convince him to help us."

With eyes wide open and eyebrows lifted I tentatively walked through the back door of the store and approached the carpenter who was banging on a stud. When he paused for a moment, I stood where he could see me and said, "Excuse me sir, do you by any chance have a saw you could lend me for a minute?"

He took one look at me and it was his turn to raise his eyebrows and ask with a smile, "What do you need it for?"

"We need to cut two pieces about this long out of the scrap two by four we found outside." I held my hands about two and a half feet apart.

"Who's we?"

"My friend Josh and me. We're making skate scooters."

He put down his hammer and picked up his Skilsaw and flipped the electric cord to permit him to go out to the back yard. "Let's go see."

Josh had pulled the stud out of the pile and had it resting with one end on the top of the heap and the other end on the ground.

"Where do you want me to cut it?"

"Here, here and here."

I barely got the words out and the pieces of wood were there on the ground for us. "Thank you so much!" I exclaimed. "Do you happen to know if Mr. Goldman has any empty orange crates inside that he doesn't need?"

"You don't miss a trick do you?" he said pleasantly. "As a matter of fact, yes, he has a bunch of them. I'm sure he won't miss a couple. Come on in, I'll show you where they are."

Josh and I were bouncing with enthusiasm as we walked back, with our orange crates and two-by-fours, to my house where we had stashed our skates to prepare to assemble our scooters. "Let's leave this stuff in the hallway while I get my mother's hammer and we can go pull nails from that same pile. I'll be right down."

Two hours later we had tapped our bent nails straight and assembled our skate scooters and were ready to roll!

Skate-scooters became our vehicles of combat during many afternoons. Two handles were attached to the top of the crate for the driver to hang onto and steer as he leaned to maneuver to train his weaponry against the "enemy" vehicles. The weaponry was multiple rubber band guns attached to the top of the orange crate. I had four guns on mine. The rubber bands were rings cut from tire inner tubes stretched along the length of the gun. When the trigger arrangement was released the rubber band would fly off

"Josh, let's go back and get another orange crate that we can break up and use the 3/4 inch thick partitions to make the bodies of the guns and the handles. We won't have to cut those pieces because they'll split easy." The rubber band ammunition was hooked over the forward end of the gun and then stretched back to be clamped in place by the trigger assembly. The trigger was a small piece of wood which was held in place by two more bands that clamped the "bullet" rubber band at the top . Pressure on the bottom of the trigger released the rubber "bullet" and let it fly because it was stretched.

"Look out, here they come out of the alley!" I hollered to Josh as I whirled around to face the attacking enemy. Danny and Wayne turned tail and we pursued as fast as we could. I was within range and let loose with one of my guns.

"Damn," I muttered when my shot missed. I pumped harder and closed the gap just a little more. And shot my number two gun. "Gotcha Danny," I shouted gleefully.

Danny was glumly muttering as he pulled over to the side. I couldn't catch up with Wayne who turned a corner into another alley and disappeared undoubtedly into one of the cellars where I couldn't follow. Josh tended to be slow and clumsy and was not good at these games requiring speed and agility. "Nice goin'," he said when I rejoined him.

"It's 4:20, we better put away our scooters and go listen to the radio," Josh continued.

"Right," I said, "Come onna my house since we're right here, OK?"

"OK".

We parked our scooters on the back porch downstairs and ran up the three floors to our apartment, dashed through the kitchen (with a "Hi Mom" on the way) and down the hall to the living room where I turned the knob on the Sears Silvertone console radio and turned the dial to WEEI. As soon as we heard the introduction to "Jack Armstrong, The All-American Boy", Josh flopped down on the floor with his hands under his chin and elbows on the floor as I draped myself over the leather hassock – and that was how we remained for the next hour and a half till the serials were over. During the whole time we lay there staring at the radio as though we could actually see what was going on. I saw all the action – in my mind.

* * *

Most of the games we played in the streets were fun with lots of camaraderie among the younger set. Manny always managed to maintain a leadership role, and in spite of his aggressive manner we were generally willing to follow along with his suggestions. Among other thing, we didn't want to be cut out of his daily milkshake routine. Every day he had a dime for a milkshake at the Cheney Drug Store that he was happy to share with us. This was one of his methods of controlling us. He always took three of his chums with him for the sharing occasion. He let each one drink as much as he was willing to permit, and then he would pinch the straw that he held while we drank.

Manny had a real mean streak which I had discovered earlier when we had our confrontations. On another occasion we were playing follow-the-leader, and of course it was Manny who was leading. But this time he arranged a very nasty trap for Wayne by not telling him what he told the rest of us.

"When we go through the alley at 30 Segel Street, in back of the building, be sure to put your feet **exactly** where I put mine, otherwise you'll have a bad surprise."

Then exercising his job as leader, he set the sequence of the followers putting Wayne at the end. Poor Wayne didn't know about the instruction to put his feet exactly where the rest of us did, and he fell into a camouflaged pit. Manny had covered the hole with branches and twigs and leaves and had been very careful to straddle the hole. When Wayne fell in everyone laughed including me. I laughed only for a moment though - when I realized what the trap was, I felt terrible. The hole in the ground was the empty concrete cylinder that normally contained a metal garbage can. But it was not empty any morel! Wayne's saucer eyes of astonishment changed to the crinkled eyes of tears, horror and humiliation as the stench enveloped him. He was standing waist deep in a foul mixture of putrifying garbage, dog shit, and rain water. While the other kids jeered, I was very distressed. I reached over and offered my hand to help him climb out.

"Wayne, there's a hose over there," I said pointing to the corner of the building. "Come on, I'll hose you off."

The hosing took care of most of the solid stuff but he still reeked as he sobbed and dripped his way home. We didn't see him for a couple months since his mother told him in no uncertain terms that he was not to play with us any more. After that, it was as though nothing happened but I'm sure he's never forgotten the experience - nor have I.

When I told Josh about what happened to Wayne, he said, "Leave it to Manny to come up with such a lousy trick!"

"I'm sure glad I wasn't the last one,"

"He wouldn't do that to you because he'd be afraid that you'd come out of that hole and beat the shit out of him again."

"I suppose so," I said, but I thought otherwise. I was thinking, given he was so much bigger than I, that without the benefit of surprise I had last time that I wouldn't be able to beat him. But then, I argued with myself, with the level of anger and adrenalin I would have had - I probably could have beaten him up. It didn't matter though because my reputation saved me from having to find out.

Chapter 9

Unfulfillment

All through grammar school, I had a crush on an adorable little girl, Charlotte. I always tried to be next to her during any class activities that allowed flexibility. I was painfully shy at the time, and hardly ever spoke to her, although I found out where she lived and made it a point to walk by her house if it was anywhere near the way I needed to go. My attraction to her went on for several years without any fulfillment, even though I walked by her house hundreds of times. She lived on the way to my grammar school, my junior high school, the Young Men's Hebrew Association and also on the way to the apartment of my stepbrother Al and his wife Glenda. Glenda's parents, the Sussewitzes, lived across the street from Charlotte, and that was a strong motivation for me to visit them often. However, an even greater motivation to visit was the fact that Glenda's mother was a fabulous baker and she loved to have me over to eat her wonderful pastries, cakes and cookies.

One day, on the way home from school, - I was nine years old at the time, - I stopped by Glenda's parents house to partake of an afternoon *nosh*, and I knocked on the front door. I was astonished when the door opened and it wasn't Glenda's mother who stood there inquiringly, it was large Negro lady. She looked at me and said questioningly, "Yes?" I looked at her, thinking that I might be in the wrong house. I glanced around and realized that, no, I was in the right place. I needed to ask for Glenda's mother but I couldn't think of her name, either the last name or the first name that I surely did not know. I was squirming as I tried to arrive at the right question to ask while this nice lady kept smiling at me and wondering what I wanted. Then I remembered that Glenda was married to my stepbrother and that made her an "in-law", and that was the basis for my visiting her mother in the first place.

So I blurted out, "Is my mother-in-law home?" This question resulted in great amusement from my greeter.

She took my hand and said, "Indeed she is. Come on in." Leading me into the kitchen she announced, "Mrs. Sussewitz, this young man wants to see his mother-in-law!"

While I was enjoying my milk and cake, Mrs. Sussewitz explained to me the basics of in-law relationships.

Despite the many opportunities, my relationship with Charlotte never got to first base.

Chapter 10

Ruthie

I was fascinated with my sister's artistic capability. With a pencil and paper she would sketch various ongoing activities and with remarkably few lines she'd capture the essence of what was happening. Everyone who saw her work was impressed and with good reason.

Despite my admiration and love for her and my appreciation for the many occasions of her watching out for my well being she definitively considered me her kid brother - the pest. In retrospect, I can't blame her. She had all these nice attractive teenage friends who came to the house, and there I was always trying to horn in on whatever they were doing. There were many times when I earned a slap in the face from Ruthie to go away and leave them alone.

I was particularly interested when she would flip through the pages of a large sketch pad showing her girl friends her drawings. What I found interesting was that she'd slam it shut whenever I came near. What kind of drawings was she doing that she didn't want me to see? I once heard her comment about the benefits of the special anatomy class that she was taking at Mass School of Art, and how it helped her drawing people. Then when I looked up the meaning of the word "anatomy" and tied it in with her closing the sketch pad whenever I came close, I figured that she must be sketching her girl friends nude. I had noticed in the art museums to which she frequently went, taking me along, that artists often liked to paint people naked - mostly ladies.

These thoughts made me more observant of what my sister did when her girl friends visited. In particular I noticed that when Gilda came, they frequently went into her bedroom and closed the door and stayed there for a long time. *Is Gilda posing naked for my sister? How can I find out? I can't peek in the window because we are three - no four- stories up. And she always had something hanging on the doorknob blocking the keyhole. I'll have to find some excuse to barge in.* I had always been very careful to knock on her door when I needed her, so Ruthie was not in the habit of locking it.

One day when Gilda and Ruthie were in the closed bedroom for a while the telephone on the little table near the door rang and I rushed to pick it up.

"Hello."

"Hi Gerry, this is Dale and I need to talk with Ruth right away."

"Hold on."

I didn't hesitate to turn the door knob as I knocked on the door and entered saying, "Ruthie, Dale wants to talk with you right away."

Sure enough, there was Gilda with nothing on and both Gilda and Ruth were screaming, "Get out of here!"

I managed to stand there pop-eyed with my jaw hanging open for several seconds as I took in the scene before me. I feigned embarrassment and slowly backed out with "I'm sorry. Excuse me. He said he wants to talk with you right away."

Just as I pulled the door closed Ruthie jerked it back open and steamed out glaring at me as if to kill as she snatched up the phone and barked into the mouthpiece, "Dale - what's so damned urgent?"

I slunk away into my bedroom and closed the door not wanting to be within earshot when she finished with Dale.

I thought about what I had seen. Gilda was the first grownup girl I ever saw with no clothes on and compared with Rachel whom I had seen just a couple years ago I thought the differences were not very big. So this lady had some titties and a bunch of hair at her crotch - so it's no big deal either. I didn't understand why people get so excited about being seen naked.

That was my nine-year-old view of the subject. I decided that my curiosity resulted from the fact that it was so hidden. Just as Rachel had said when I was seven.

After Gilda left I got one helova slap in the face and lecture about respecting privacy and "Don't you EVER come into my room again without being told to enter after you knock!"

Ruthie was always quick with her slaps when she thought I needed them - which of course was a lot more often than I thought I did. She was quite athletic and strong and I was no match for her when I tried hard to fight back. She always managed to grab my arm and hold it so that I couldn't hit her. That's the way it was until December 31, 1935.

I don't remember what sparked her wrath that afternoon but she was giving me a real going over. I managed to get my right arm free from her grasp. I twisted around, made a fist and swung as hard as I could and caught her full on the mouth.

"Yow - that hurt!" she yelped.

"What do you think your slaps feel like?" I answered back as she released my other arm and stopped hitting me. I felt very good about having landed one since I had never been able to do that before. But when I looked at her lip as it started to swell, I felt a little less good about it. Then later when she tearfully called Dale to cancel their New Years Eve date because she wouldn't be seen with a fat lip - I felt terrible.

But you know something, she never, - ever - hit me again.

Chapter 11

More Kid Philosophy

During the next several years, Josh and his parents never tired of trying to convert me to some degree of Jewish piety, and we two precocious youngsters continued our philosophic discussions. When I was 11 years old in 1936, we were again walking on Blue Hill avenue by Franklin Park, and Josh asked, "If there's no God, how come there is such a thing as love and all the other emotions that people feel? Don't you think that someone or something would have to arrange for them to be there?"

I wrinkled my forehead and thought for a few moments, and then answered, "Maybe those emotions evolved too as people developed and they found that they needed them in order to get along with each other and to survive. Especially love, I think I heard somewhere that love is what makes the earth go round – not really – that love is what makes sure that the populations grow. It works for animals too, they mate to make more animals. Fear is another one of those emotions that helps keep the animals alive, and I suppose people too."

"I heard that too," Josh replied, "but I also heard that it was money that makes the earth go round. Love and money – what a combination! Every movie we see seems to have one or both themes.

Every book too. Hate too. I guess we can call that negative love I suppose. But getting back to God, don't you think that he had something to do with it?"

"Naw, why couldn't it be that only those people and animals survived that had those emotions? I don't know how hate could contribute to their survival, but the other two, yes. On the subject of hate, if there is a God, why would he let people hate each other?"

"God made people with the ability to think for themselves and to do whatever they want. As a matter of fact, all the evil in the world comes from that, you know, from people not from God." Josh gestured animatedly and dramatically, pointing at his head when he said "think for themselves" and spreading his arms at the "evil in the world".

"But Josh, when he saw what a mess that made, why didn't he change it? If he is all-powerful, why couldn't he remove the capability to do evil from man? After all, he was supposed to have designed him in the first place. People pray for all kinds of things, I'm sure that eliminating poverty and violence must be among the things they pray for – so he must know about those things – he cannot claim ignorance – besides he's supposed to know everything, isn't that so?"

"Would you like it if you couldn't do what you wanted to do?"

"There are all kinds of things that we cannot do! Look at all the laws we have against this and that. We cannot legally kill each other unless we are the government! They killed Sacco and Vanzetti even though there were all kinds of claims that they didn't do what they were supposed to have done." I was parroting what I had heard my mother and her communist friends talking about on that subject.

"I don't know about Sacco and Vanzetti, but I do know that God doesn't want to impose limitations on all of us!"

"How do you know that?"

"Because he hasn't done it. And I know that he could if he wanted to."

"Then he certainly isn't benevolent is he?"

"He is too. He only punishes those who deserve it."

"Come on, Josh! What about little children who suffer when they haven't even been around long enough to do anything evil?"

"He's got his reasons. Maybe he's punishing their parents – I don't know."

"I don't know either, but that's one of the reasons I don't accept that there is a God."

* * *

If their parents could have heard the discussions, they would have been astonished at how these two pre-teenagers continued to tackle these profound problems that have stumped society for so many years before that time. Evolution versus creationism – not something new in the 1930's or since. Benevolent versus all-powerful god, also not a new subject, and also not one usually discussed by such young people. Gerry and Joshsua were fascinated by their discussions, especially when they got onto the subject of time.

"Gerry, when the bible describes the days when God created the earth and all that, he didn't necessarily mean that each day was just one of our days long. His days could have been weeks, or even years long – we cannot take them literally. But not millions of years like Darwin says."

"Josh, do you think that God created all the skies and stars and planets and our sun too?"

"Yes I do."

"Josh, you've heard of a lightyear haven't you? You know that is about 6 trillion miles. And I recently read that the new 200 inch telescope they've built in California is seeing stars that are millions of lightyears away, and when you look up into the sky, we see millions of stars. Can you imagine how many stars are up there? I cannot imagine it, but I know that it is a huge number. Do you think that God invented all of them and is listening to prayers from all the beings that may be on some of them? Josh, it makes no sense to me to even think that there is something other than nature responsible for all of it." I stopped waving my arms as I finished the last sentence.

Chapter 12

Move to Dorchester and Back

"I fund us a nice apartment to rent in Dorchester. It's a flat on de toid floor in a nice neighborhood near Morton Street and near de G&G deli too," Sol Samuels announced one evening at dinner. "De landlord here raised de rent too much so ve hef to move in July." There was no discussion.

This happened at the end of May, 1938 and I was sure that the timing was chosen to accommodate my finishing the eighth grade at the Theodore Roosevelt Junior High School in Roxbury I was now 12 years old and almost at my full height of 5'6" and I carried about 145 pounds of muscle. My Friend Josh at 14 was 6'2" and weighed more than 200 pounds. Josh and I were already familiar with that part of Dorchester because we had frequently walked there past Franklin Park and Franklin Field and we had several times purchased ice cream at the G&G. The deli was a favorite gathering spot for the Jewish men of the area, so much so, that the politicians used to come there to give speeches hoping for the Jewish vote. I had no concern about the move causing me to lose my friends, because it wasn't so far away.

The house at 23 Hansborough Street was an older wooden building with gray peeling paint and three porches facing the street.

At one end of the street was the Mass State Hospital that we called the Mad House, and at the other end was Blue Hill Avenue, the main drag from Mattapan, through Dorchester and Roxbury. Our move into the house was routine. However, my entry into the Solomon Lewenberg Junior High School for the 9th grade, turned out to be far from routine.

As a transferee, I was assigned a counselor who invited me into his office. "Hi Gerald, I'm Mr. Helfman and you are assigned to me for guidance. I see from your records that you were in the Rapid Advancement program - that's good. Good grades too. No discipline problems - excellent. Now, what course are you thinking of taking?"

"I'd like to take a college preparatory course."

"Why?"

"I want to go to college."

"Why?"

"Because I think I can get a better job if I have a college education."

"Do you know how much money you need to go to college? Does your family have money?"

"No."

"What do you want to study in college?"

"I don't know."

"You don't know what you want to study in college, and you have no prospect of having the money to go. No, you won't take a college course; you'll take a commercial course. Here's the list of courses you'll take. You'll find it easier than the college course, - you'll study bookkeeping instead of algebra."

I shrugged and took the papers thinking about how I didn't like the way Mr. Helfman had pushed me into a commercial course, but how I did like the idea of not having to take algebra - I had heard that it was a tough course. But he really didn't give me a choice.

* * *

My home room teacher, Miss Tryano, assigned me the desk in the first row on the right aisle, near the front door of the classroom. From there I could easily see her when she sat at her desk and better yet when she stood in front of the desk. I enjoyed watching her, because she was very good looking and she had a cute body which was easily seen because of the revealing clothes she wore. She never had a problem keeping the attention of the 9th grade boys - most of whom were awash in new hormones and becoming conscious of their sexuality. But, I was not yet aware of that aspect of growing up.

I didn't understand why I was so distracted when she sometimes stood at the corner of my desk while she gave some of her talks. She often leaned forward over my desk resting her crotch on the corner - that used to drive me bananas. I often lost track of the lecture when she did that, although I tried to appear to be taking notes. I never figured out whether she did that purposely to titillate me and the other boys, or whether she had an itch or whether she was masturbating. At that time, however, I didn't know the meaning of that word.

* * *

I had heard from older boys the term "jerk-off" used in several different contexts, none of which I understood. As a verb, I once heard one of the boys say to another, "Aw why don't you go jerk off." It was not a question. In another instance, I heard someone use it as a noun, that is, "Oh he's such a jerk-off." And then I'd also heard that shortened to "Oh he's such a jerk." I was mystified by these terms. I knew that the word "jerk" meant a short quick motion but I made no connection with anything else I knew.

One morning, I awoke as usual and went into the bathroom to pee. As I stood in front of the toilet pointing my penis, I noticed that it felt strangely firm. In addition as much as I felt like I needed to pee, it felt better if I didn't - so I realized that I was holding it back. I squeezed it to help holding back the urine. When the pressure was about to become too great, I squeezed it again - and I was astounded by what happened next! I couldn't hold it back any longer and as my knees buckled and my hips thrusted rapidly forward and back, a high energy, white, sticky stream of something squirted from my penis and splattered against the toilet lid, and the back wall. My bewilderment and absolute panic at what had happened was tamed by the fantastically pleasurable sensations I had experienced.

As I mopped up the mess with toilet paper, it suddenly hit me - that that was what the older boys were talking about when they talked about jerking off! I had just done it and I loved it! Wow! I had discovered a great entertainment that was completely within my control! Fantastic! From that day forward, I always managed to find time to jerk-off.

* * *

A few weeks later, I was invited to join Josh and his group of older boys at a Saturday night party at Billy's house. He told me how his parents helped out with his parties.

"Mom, I'll be home late tonight, so don't worry about me. You don't have to wait up until I come home. We're having a little Saturday night party at Billy's house. His parents are great to us, they not only provide *nosherei*, but they also participate in our games and our dancing. As a matter of fact, Billy's father plays the piano for us."

Although I didn't know several of the girls, I nevertheless enjoyed the evening. After dancing and eating, each of us settled down with one of the girls on the sofa or in an easy chair for necking or in my inexperienced case, just for conversation. Billy's mother and father did the same thing. It was almost 1:00 AM on Sunday morning by the time I got home, and I could see that my mother's door was slightly ajar so that she could see when I came in. In those days it was comparatively safe for a mature 13 year old boy to be out at that hour.

I went into the bathroom, washed my hands, peed, changed into my pajamas and dropped my dirty underwear and shirt into the laundry hamper in the hallway just outside my room and went to bed.

The next morning, my mother heard me getting dressed after I had slept late and she was waiting for me when I came out the door heading for the bathroom.

"Gerry! Vot kind of goils vere at your party lest night?" she asked pointedly.

I looked at her wondering what she was concerned about. "Nice girls, Ma. Why do you ask?"

"I'm esking because I vant to know vy your undershorts hev lipstick around de fly!" She was waving my undershorts under my nose pointing at red stains around the fly. She found them while preparing the laundry.

I looked at the lipstick in consternation. How in the world could lipstick get there without my knowing? I did have a drink last night, but I knew that I wasn't drunk, and if I had gotten a blow job from someone, I would certainly have noticed! Would I ever! After I learned about hard-ons and jerking off first hand, I asked lots of questions of my boy friends and learned with great interest about fucking and blow jobs.

I was shaking my head slowly right and left as I reached for the undershorts to see the lipstick more closely. As my right hand reached the shorts I saw what it was all about and I dissolved into hysterical laughter. I couldn't stop laughing while my mother was first astonished and then angry that I didn't give her a straight answer - but I couldn't talk, I was laughing so hard. Finally I simmered down enough to be able to say "Mercurochrome!" pointing to the water-stained band aid covering a scratch on my finger. When I got home from the party, I washed my hands and then peed, thereby putting the red on my underwear.

My mother smiled sheepishly and patted me on the head and went into the kitchen to make me a nice breakfast.

* * *

At the end of the school year, we moved back to Roxbury because Mr. Samuels had found a nice apartment on the first floor of a house on Warren Street for lower rent than he was paying for the third floor in Dorchester. It also had a big yard. It was also a predominantly Jewish neighborhood.

I was pleased because it was only two blocks from Roxbury Memorial High School where I'd be going in the fall. I should say Roxbury Memorial High School FOR BOYS because there was no such thing as co-ed education in Boston at that time. The building was a long red brick structure divided into three parts. The boy's school was on the left and the girl's school was on the right, and the library was in the middle. Both sexes were permitted to use the library, but there was very close supervision and talking was limited to whispering and that was discouraged especially between the genders. Guards were stationed at the doors leading to the girl's school preventing entry by any boy.

When school started, I registered for the college preparatory course and I was surprised to find how many different classes I had to take. That also meant that I was always carrying a very heavy book bag filled to overflowing. On Friday afternoon of my third week at the school, after school let out, I left the library about a half hour after everyone else had gone, and started to walk home down Townsend street toward Warren Street. I was walking at a leisurely pace when I suddenly noticed that halfway between the gate to the library and Warren Street, a distance of about 50 yards, there were four boys leaning against the fence seemingly chatting innocently. I was immediately alarmed because I had heard that there had been several incidents in which hoodlums from Irish South Boston came to the Jewish neighborhoods looking for lone kids to beat up, and I wondered if I was about to become one of those kids.

I maintained my leisurely pace as though I had not seen them although my heart was thumping like a jackhammer, and I kept my head down as though I was watching where I was walking. *Should I turn around and run back to the library? But if I do that, will they be waiting for me when I come out? With my heavy book bag, I'll not be able to run fast enough anyway - they could still catch me. Or I could cross the street - but that wouldn't stop them if they were after me.* As I debated with myself what to do, with my head still down but my eyes up, I had been watching them and when one of them almost imperceptibly nodded his head in my direction and then two of them changed position from the fence to the curb forcing me to walk between the two pairs, I knew that the pending attack was real.

By then, it was too late to do anything but continue walking toward them, which I did with my head down as though I had not noticed them. I was building an incredible head of adrenalin as my survival instincts took over. Just before I reached them, gripping the cord of my book bag with my right hand, I knocked the bag to my left with my right elbow and I twisted my body in the same direction and as the boy on my left started to reach for me, I uncoiled away from him to the right swinging the heavy book bag as in a hammer throw catching the boy by the fence on the side of his head, knocking him into the boy beside him, and they both went down. With an incredibly loud "KAYAAH!", I elbowed the boy on my left in the solar plexus and he fell off the curb and then I swung my right toe up into the crotch of the remaining open-mouthed attacker. Then with all four of them on the ground I ran like hell towards Warren street ignoring the fact that my heavy bag should have slowed me down - it didn't. They were in no shape to pursue me so I arrived at home breathless but unscathed - and laughing hysterically. *I can't believe I pulled that off! I can't believe it! I guess the key to my success was surprise because they didn't know that I had seen them and that I was so energized by being so scared. Damn but I was scared! I remember reading about some of the terrible things that happened to some other Jewish kids. One kid was stabbed and another one lost an eye and another one was still in a coma. And then there was that case in Grove Hall where a kid had his face bashed in with a brick while a friggin' cop watched and did nothing! Boy am I lucky!*

Suddenly my glee faded as I realized that these four would be waiting for me on Monday and that I would not have the advantage of surprise and they would have the advantage of anger and revenge. *How can I survive on Monday afternoon when the four of them are bound to be waiting for me. If I had a gang of friends in the school, we could probably have a fair fight - but I don't have a gang. I've only been in the school three weeks. I'll have to find another way to equalize the fight.*

I thought all that Friday evening and Saturday morning before I hit on an approach that would enable me to survive the four against one situation. I reached into the right rear corner of the top drawer of my dresser and removed $4.50 that I had saved in the glass peanut butter jar. I strapped on my roller skates and went down Quincy street to Blue Hill Avenue and around the corner to the pawn shop. There was a tray full of knives of various sizes, different styles, and prices all over the lot.

"Excuse me, Sir. I'm looking for a switchblade knife that'll fit in my pocket and not cost too much."

"Perhaps one of these four will work for you."

After snapping each knife several times and observing the action and feeling the weight, I selected one with a sharp four-inch blade that worked well and cost only $2.75. This was going to be my equalizer.

On Monday after classes, I left all my books in the locker and went out the gate unencumbered to walk down Townsend Street again. I had waited until most of the crowd had left so the sidewalk was not congested so it would be easier to spot the foursome if they were there. It took only a moment to see them more or less in the same place they were last time. I again feigned not seeing them and walked towards them with my head down looking at the ground. Just before I reached them, I took out the knife, snapped it open and proceeded to clean my finger nails with the point. As I came abreast of them, I looked each one aggressively in the eyes and continued past them turning and walking backwards just a few steps and stopped, still with the knife in hand, I said,

"And don't come back."

I heaved a sigh of relief when I saw them walk away.

* * *

The year before, Mr. Helfin had told me that algebra was a tough course, but when I got into it, I found it easy and I loved it. As a matter of fact, I found all the tenth grade courses easy. I developed a format for doing the homework assigned in a class during the next class so I only had maybe one homework to do at home at the end of the day and frequently I managed to do the last one during the last class.

"Gerry, I never see you doing any homework. Don't you have any assignments?" Ruthie asked.

"Sure I have homework assignments - but I do them before I come home."

"You can't do all your homework before you get home. Then it's not homework."

"How about calling them additional work assignments - which I can do anywhere."

"Don't be a wiseass, - you're going to fail if you don't do your homework! How do you think you'll be able to go to college with lousy grades."

"Quit bugging me - I'll show you my report card when I get it!"

When I brought home almost all A's she stopped nagging me about my homework.

One day though, my skill at algebra got me in trouble during a mid-term exam. I had heard several of the boys talking quietly about their crib sheets and their tricks for being able to look at them without getting caught. I thought the most ingenious one was the idea of writing the needed information on the underside of a necktie which could be read when the wearer leaned forward and the tie rested on the desk with the underside visible. If the teacher came near, the wearer only had to straighten up and the tie would fall into its normal position on the chest with the cheating evidence hidden. Fortunately, I didn't feel the need for cheating so I ignored those discussions.

"OK now, everybody put all your books and papers into the desks out of sight, and I'll distribute the test. You'll have 45 minutes and when I say pencils down, you will put them down immediately. If you don't, you will be penalized." When the thumping of all the desk-tops stopped, he continued, "I am passing out the tests upside down, and that is how they are to stay on your desks until I tell you to start."

"OK, now start."

I flipped over the test paper and started to do the problems along with everyone else. I worked feverishly to finish before the 45 minutes were up. I finished the problems and realized that it had gone quickly and that I had time to check my work. I went through every problem and was satisfied that I had done them correctly. Then I looked up at the wall clock and realized that only 15 minutes had gone by. *How will I spend the remaining 30 minutes. I can't stare at my paper for that long and I can't look around the room because the teacher'll think I'm looking at someone else's paper. I'll just look at the teacher so he'll see that my eyes are not wandering over someone's shoulder to see his paper.* The teacher walked back and forth at the front on the room, and my head followed him. I noticed that he looked at me kinda funny as he kept walking and I kept looking at him. Then he went up the left aisle of the room towards the back and I turned my eyes down to my paper rather than continue to follow him.

Suddenly he was on my right gripping my shoulder with his left hand and shoving his face into mine and hissing "Are you cheating?" Before I could say anything, he had grabbed my tie with his right hand and looked at the underside.

"N - no, I'm not cheating sir, I'm finished and I don't know where to look. Here, take my paper." The paper was rattling from my trembling hand.

He took the paper, glanced at it and said, "Sit there." He went with the paper back to his desk at the front of the room. I was still bored, but at least I could look wherever I wanted. When I saw how the rest of the class was working so intensely to finish what I had found so simple I realized how lucky I was to have had such an affinity for algebra.

Chapter 13

Summer Vacation

"Ve're going to Oak Island for summer vacation," my mother announced one evening during supper. "Ve haf a nice cottage near de beach vid tree bedrooms. Rutie and Rose vill be togedder vid a cot for Selly ven she can come. De boys vill have a bedroom too for ven dey can come. And Gerry vil sleep outside on de porch."

"On the porch?!" I exclaimed.

"Don't vorry, Gerreleh, it is screened in and you'll have a nice comftible bed."

Mr. Samuels had rented the cottage for the two months of July and August during this year of 1938. With all of his children working and contributing to the household, enough money had been saved to permit us the luxury of escaping some of the summer heat and humidity of Boston. For my mother, Ruthie, cousin Rose and me it would be a full time vacation, because none of us worked. For the others, it would be mostly on weekends, although Sol was going to commute back and forth each day. The commute wasn't bad, considering that the narrow gage railway from Point of Pines to East Boston via Revere Beach, made its first stop at Oak Island, and the ferry across the harbor dropped him off at Rowes Wharf, within walking distance of the factory where he worked.

The Factor family, including cousin Rose were all grinning happily at the prospect, while the Samuels children were quite expressionless, clearly not happy with their apparent second class position. But, on the other hand, they were also pleased at the prospect of having a nice weekend destination at the beach.

Cousin Rose had been living with us during the last eight months, since her father, my Uncle Frank, with his new wife had moved to California leaving her alone in the east. She worked intermittently, but she was unemployed for the summer.

* * *

Our move-in on July 1st went smoothly and after I helped carry in some of the bedding and food, I spent the next hour looking around our cottage and the neighborhood. The gray clapboard cottages were lined up on one side of the street, which was mostly dirt. On the other side of the street were wetlands with meandering sloughs. With the tide high at that time, the water in the sloughs was just below ground level; they were between six to eight feet wide. A short distance away, I could see a little bridge over a section of a slough, and there were three boys playing in the water and obviously having lots of fun.

"Hi," I said as I arrived at the bridge. "Are you here for the summer, or do you live here all the time?"

"I'm just for the summer," the red headed lad replied.

"Same here," from the square looking kid.

The third boy had his head under water and hadn't heard the question.

"I'm here for the summer too. My name's Gerry Factor, what's yours?"

"I'm Eddy, some people call me Red, he's John, and the other one is Bud. Come on in, the water's great."

"Not wearing a bathing suit, just got here. How deep's the water?"

John replied, "Five to seven feet. Right here it's about six feet. You don't want to dive straight down or you can get stuck in the mud. Where do ya live?"

"I live in Roxbury."

"I mean here, what number Oak Island Lane?"

"Oh, we're staying in number 24."

"We're next door neighbors! We are in number 26. We're from Everett. John lives a couple houses further down in number 32. Bud lives a block over on Pine Street."

"Is the water always this deep, or does it go up and down with the tides?", I asked.

"When the tide goes out, there's no water at all - it goes down to the mud! "Eddy replied. "Tide'll be ok for swimming for about three more hours, then it'll get kinda shallow."

"Great! I'm gonna head home and get my bathing suit."

As I was leaving, Eddy continued with, "When the high tide is near sundown we go bollikey."

I stopped and turned around, " Bollikey? What's bollikey?"

"That's skinney-dipping - you know we swim naked. It's especially fun when the girls show up!"

"That sure sounds interesting." I said wide-eyed. "When's the next time the sunset's going to be right?"

"Don't know for sure, but I think its still a week or so away. "

Fantastic! I said to myself as I walked off. I was VERY interested in swimming with naked girls! As a matter of fact, even though I was now 12 years old, I had not seen a naked girl since I had played "I'll show you mine if you'll show me yours" with Greenbaum's daughter ages ago when I was seven. My interest had definitely grown in the past several months when my voice had changed and my testicles had descended and my pubic hair had appeared and I had learned about wet dreams and masturbating. Oh yes I was looking forward to bollikey swimming!

When I jumped into the water I was delighted at how clear it was and how the temperature felt so good. "This sure beats swimming in the ocean!" I exclaimed.

"Yeah, I agree. The only thing missing is the waves." Eddy replied.

"Can't ride the waves when there ain't none, but on the other hand for swimming, its hard to beat," Bud added.

Eddy appeared to be about the same age as I, perhaps a little less muscular, but about the same size. His bushy head of red hair was what attracted attention to him most often.

"Where do you live", I asked.

"Malden. I'm here with my Mom and Dad. This is the third year we've rented this cottage for the summer. We just love it here."

"What do your folks do when you're here?"

"My Mom bakes in the sun all day on the beach, and my Dad commutes into Boston every day. He works in a machine shop. He buys a monthly pass for the narrow guage train that goes to East Boston, and then he takes the ferry across to Rowes Wharf and from there he walks to work."

"My stepfather does the same thing - not in a machine shop, but I don't know whether he buys a monthly pass or not," I said.

"Say, how old are you?"

"I'm twelve, will be thirteen in September. How old are you?"

"I was thirteen in May. Boy am I glad you showed up! Let me tell you why. My father uses his train pass during the week, and on the weekend he lets me use it. Now, get this: The pass is good for one adult and one child. An adult is anyone over twelve, and twelve and under is a child. This is terrific, I'm the adult and you're the child and we can ride the train and ferry all day long if we want - I'm tired of going alone - it's boring with no one to talk to and help enjoy it. John and Bud are both fourteen. How about trying it next weekend?"

"You bet! That sounds like a lotta fun."

That night, after supper, I was thinking about how wonderful this vacation was going to be. Here I am with a screened in porch essentially to myself at the ocean, away from the city heat, with three nice kids already identified for friends, a great swimming hole, a wonderful beach nearby, and prospects for free train and ferry rides, and even the possibility of swimming with naked girls. I was in seventh heaven - whatever that was supposed to mean. Speaking of naked girls, I wondered if I could peek through the window into the room where my sister and cousin Rose were going to sleep and maybe see them naked too. I was lying on my cot that was against the wall directly below their window. I knew that Ruthy and Rose were still sitting in the kitchen listening to the radio that came with the cottage but I could at least see whether the shade was up a little. I got up on my knees which brought my eyes perfectly even with the window sill and joy of joys there was a gap of about one quarter of an inch through which I could see the entire room although just barely because it was dark with only a little light spilling in from the kitchen.

I was worn out from the activities of the day, and I really wanted to sleep, but I knew if I went to sleep I would miss my sister and cousin getting undressed. I kept myself awake by deep breathing and thinking of all kinds of things. Finally about 10:30, the light went on in the girls room, and that quarter inch became a brilliant strip and I started to maneuver myself into position to look in, when it suddenly went dark as I saw two fingers on the bottom pulling the shade down flush with the sill. Damn! They knew I'd be peeking if there was any crack through which to look. I momentarily contemplated complaining to them that they were being insulting to me with their assumptions, but I decided against it.

* * *

"Do you have some kind of identification that'll prove that you're twelve years old? You'll need that tomorrow if we're going to ride that train and ferry," Eddy told me.

"I think my mother has a copy of my birth certificate. I'll ask her for it."

"Vat are you goink to do? You're goink to ride de tren and de ferry? Who's dis adult Eddy? I vant to meet him. Come you sed he lives in number twenty-six.. She took my hand and dragged me next door to where Eddy lived and knocked on the door. I was mortified but deep down I knew she was looking out for my welfare. Eddy opened the door.

"Hi Eddy, I want you to meet my mother."

"Hi Mrs. Factor."

"Tell me 'ow you ride the tren and ferry."

After repeating the story about the child and adult requirements on the train, Eddy said, " I've already done it twice this summer and I went all the way across the harbor and back. It's a great ride and it doesn't cost anything! My father says that I can have the pass for the whole weekend- every weekend."

My mother was satisfied that Eddy seemed to be a nice kid, and that the use of the pass was legitimate and she gave me the proof of my age and permission to go.

We boarded the train the next morning with no challenges at all and took seats by the window on the left side of the car. Eddy explained, "Going towards Boston, the left side is more interesting. Coming back, it's the right side." Shortly after we got going, the conductor came through with a punch dangling from his belt asking for tickets. When he came to us Eddy showed him the pass and the conductor look at me and said,

"How old are you?"

"I'm twelve."

He looked at me for a moment and moved on.

"He already knows me." Eddy volunteered.

Initially the view from the train was of the backsides of the stores along the beach and then there was a short stretch of residential areas. Next we were traveling along the edge of Winthrop bay looking across at the boats and houses. Off to the right we could see the water tower on Winthrop Heights and beyond that we could see Deer Island and the prison. I was familiar with Winthrop from the previous summer visits we had been there. Then all of a sudden we were treated to the sight of an American Airlines DC3 taking off from the East Boston Airport. It seemed so huge as it was still very low when it flew almost over the train. The stops to pick up passengers were very short. The speeds between stops seemed fast and the clickety-clack of the rails was mesmerizing. I was completely fascinated with the scenery and so was Eddy even though he had seen it many times. Then the waterfront and airport were gone and we were in commercial East Boston.

"This part of the trip is kinda dull, but it gets interesting again when we come to the harbor and ferry which is very soon," Eddy explained.

The train slowed and pulled into a huge shed. As we entered, I could see a lineup of cars waiting to drive onto the ferry that wasn't there yet.

"Gee, I didn't realize that the ferry took cars too," I said.

We got off the train and walked to the pedestrian waiting area that was located to the side of the ramp for the cars. Looking towards the harbor in between the two slanted walls of what looked like telephone poles tied together, I could see the skyline of Boston and the ferry heading directly toward us. I expected the ferry to slow down as it neared the entrance to the dock where we were waiting, but all it did was cut the engines and coast, it didn't do an engine reverse. I saw that it wasn't perfectly lined up to enter the telephone pole nest and I was surprised to see that as the edge of the ferry contacted the wall it moved back and gently slowed the ferry until it contacted the other wall which also moved back and it gently came to a stop with its bow at the edge of the ramp. A crew member dropped the chain in front of the double line of the cars, and as soon as the ramp was lowered they started driving off. There was a separate exit beside the automobile ramp for pedestrians. When all the cars and passengers were off, the waiting cars started to drive on and Eddy said, "Come on Gerry, let's go up to the passenger deck and get away from all this exhaust.

We went out onto the open deck that ran along the edge of the superstructure. The fresh sea air was tainted by exhaust and the smell of creosote and tar that covered the telephone poles. When all the people and cars were aboard, three blasts of the whistle signaled that the ferry was about to leave. I hadn't noticed that the captain of the ferry had moved from his front bridge to one at the other end and when it pulled out, the ship had a new bow. Approximately twenty minutes later we arrived at Rowes Wharf and the process of landing, loading and leaving was repeated.

"Eddy, what's that nice smell?"

"That's the coffee packing plant. It's only a block away," he said pointing towards a building in the direction of South Boston. We stayed on board for the ride back and enjoyed the exhilarating air and the views of islands and skylines and ships in the harbor.

Back on the train, listening to the rhythm of the klickety-klack of the wheels on the tracks reminded me of the state: of connec'-ticut-connec'-ticut-connec'-ticut pronouncing all of the c's.

I slept very well that evening after I checked that the blind was all the way down and that I couldn't see a thing in the girls' room.

* * *

The twilight produced a mystic feeling and fascinating reflections in the still water as the current stopped and the tide changed from incoming to ebb. The only sound other than the crickets and cicadas was the lap of the water as it was gently disturbed by the four of us swimming along the slough first upstream and then back down.

"Where are the girls?" I asked.

"They should be along soon, but they usually wait until it's a little darker," Eddy replied.

"Aw shit, I don't think they're coming - it's almost 8:30 and it's starting to get pretty dark already," John said.

We were all bollikey and enjoying the sensuous feeling of the cool water on our entire bodies including those parts usually covered by our swim suits.

Suddenly Bud exclaimed, "I think I see them coming. Yep that's them and they're walking towards us. It's Susan and June.'

We watched as they drew closer and then Eddy greeted them with, "Hi Sue, hi June. Nice to see you again. Come on in, the water's great. You know Bud and John, - this is Gerry."

"Hi, glad to meet you," I said.

They were now standing on the little bridge peering at me as I was at them to see what we looked like so that maybe we might recognize each other if we met in the daytime. They were carrying towels and wearing bathing suits and I was trying to assess what they might look like when they took them off. They looked awful young, and I was beginning to doubt that they had breasts yet. They stood there for just a moment or two and they dropped their suits on the bridge and dove into the water. During that very brief moment I managed to see that they had itty bitty titties starting to show, and that they had just a little bit of pubic hair. I guessed that they were about 12 years old, just like me, but maybe not yet quite as progressed into puberty. Their hips were pretty straight too and I was thinking that this was going to be less that the hoped for experience. On the other hand, I didn't really know what I was hoping for. I guess I was hoping to see a fully developed female naked.

We all were passable swimmers, and whenever one of us approached one of the girls in the water, we'd hear, "Ok, that's close enough." In the dark water, there was absolutely nothing to be seen and clearly there wasn't to be any touching or feeling. We all took turns climbing out of the water onto the bridge to dive back in, but the sun went down and the moon had not yet risen so our views of each other were all very fuzzy in the disappearing twilight. It turned out to be a very casual, pleasant, non-sexy, nude evening - pleasant but disappointing.

I saw Susan and June many time during the day swimming in the slough and also at the beach; they were very nice, but no special friendships developed. I also went with Eddy three more times on the train-ferry ride and the last time was boring. All in all, the swimming was great and the summer galloped along.

* * *

I frequently walked with Eddy along the "boardwalk" which was really a concrete road to Revere Beach and out onto the pier. There were always lots of people fishing from the pier, but the real interesting part for me was out at the end where people lined up to get a fifteen minute ride in a little seaplane. The plane would take off and climb to some low altitude and then fly over Oak Island, Point of Pines and Nahant Beach and then back to land on the water near the pier and pick up another three passengers and do it again. The plane looked like an enclosed boat hull with a wing and a tail and a pusher propeller engine in back of the wing. The wing had floats at each end to prevent them from getting into the water. When it was waiting for passengers, the plane was hooked up to a buoy about 50 yard from the pier. The fellow who sold the tickets also rowed the boat with the passengers to the plane. The rides cost fifty cents.

"I'm fascinated by airplanes," I confided to Eddy.

"Me too."

"I'm making a scrap book of all the different kinds of planes. I have lots of pictures of the World War airplanes and also some of the racing planes. and also a picture of the spirit of St. Louis that

Lindbergh flew to Paris. And I've got a terrific shot of a silver DC3, the American Airlines passenger airliner! Remember, we've seen that one take off from the East Boston Airport."

"Yah, I remember."

"That seaplane I think is made by Grumman, but I'm not sure. I'd give anything to get a ride on that, but fifty cents is out of my class."

"Not me! I'd be scared." Eddy said. "But you know something, since you know how to row, I bet if you offered that guy who's running the show, that you'd row the passengers out to the plane for him that he'd give you a ride."

I looked at Eddy with a big smile. "Eddy, you're a genius! I'm going to try that."

"Excuse me sir, I see that you spend a lot of time rowing your passengers out to the plane, wouldn't things go faster and easier for you if you let me do that for you?"

"I can't afford to hire anyone, sorry."

"I'm not looking to get paid."

"You're not?"

"All I ask is when you have only two passenger for a flight, that you give me a free ride."

"Hmm. Let me see how well you can handle the rowboat."

My enthusiasm was boundless as I jumped into the boat, grabbed the oars and proceeded to show Steve - that was the name on his shirt - the things I had learned about rowing the year before at Canoby Lake. It was a big rowboat capable to taking six passengers plus the rower but I had no difficulty taking it out a short distance and then spinning it around and returning for a perfect gentle docking maneuver.

"OK, you are our new shuttle to the plane!"

The first time I took passengers to the plane, I realized that it was bigger than I thought. I was thrilled to have the deplaning passengers step from the plane onto the boat and then the departing passengers vice versa. During the first week, there was no occasion when there were only two passengers, however on Tuesday of the second week there was an available seat. Steve said, "Gerry, take the two passengers and the pilot to the plane and tie the boat to the buoy and you sit in the copilot's seat and you'll get your free ride." There were no deplaning passengers because the plane had been waiting for several hours with no customers.

"You bet!" was my reply.

"Everyone's seat belt fastened?" Tommy asked as he started the engine. Everyone nodded, because it was so noisy, no one could hear anything but the engine. Tommy opened the door on his side and grabbed the rope that tied us to the buoy and untied it from the plane letting it fall into the water. He revved up the engine and we taxied away from the buoy and the rowboat. He turned into the wind and hollered into my ear that we'd have to wait for the engine to warm up some more before we can take off. After a couple minutes he pointed at the temperature gauge and nodded and then he gradually pushed the throttle forward and the plane slowly picked up speed. The plane was plowing through the water and not going fast at all. Then we felt it rise up and the hull started to plane on the water, and then we were airborne. I was excited by my first time in the air and my head was swiveling right, front, left, front, right - I had to see everything there was to see.

I looked at the altitude gauge and saw that we had leveled off at 3000 feet and that we were flying parallel to the beach towards Oak Island. From here I could see that a slough like the one we had been swimming in was what made it an island, and I could also see how the slough connected to the Pine River and the ocean tides. In the distance I could see the narrow gauge railroad Eddy and I had ridden to Boston. Soon we were over Point of Pines and turning right towards the Nahant peninsular. Then we were over Nahant and turning right again back toward where we came from. In the distance I could see the pier and as we drew closer I could see the buoy and the rowboat waiting for us. Then we were losing altitude preparing to land on the water. As the water came up to us, I expected to hear a swishing sound as the hull contacted the little ripples and waves below us. Instead, I was terrified by the thunderous pow, bang, thump, thump as the hull hit the water with only the thickness of the sheet metal below our feet. The impacts and vibrations were like a crash! We strained against our seat belts at the sudden slowing when the hull stopped planing and became a boat again plowing through the water. Tommy was completely relaxed so I concluded that this was perfectly normal - which of course it was. When we were again moored to the buoy and back in the rowboat, I said, "Tommy, that was fantastic! Thanks for the ride."

I finished the second week rowing for Steve, and then told him I had to quit because we were going back to Roxbury in a few days and I had to help pack up.

* * *

For the first six weeks that we were there, the girls were religious about making sure that the blind was adequately pulled down so that I could not peek. But one day during week seven, they did indeed pull it down, but in so doing they pulled it slightly sideways so that there was a vertical strip at the edge that was open about one sixteenth of an inch. Small but adequate if I put my eye right up close, which I was not reluctant to do. Of course the screen was a slight impediment, but I managed.

I could see that my sister was already asleep, while voluptuous cousin Rose was about to undress right in front of me. She pulled up her dress over her head, and I saw that she was wearing a brassiere but no underpants. I was fascinated with the view of her pubic hair as she unhooked her bra. Then she put her leg up on a chair to roll down her stockings and as she leaned over, I saw that her large breasts were wide at the end with the nipple, and that they necked down where they were attached to her chest. Kinda like a rubber balloon filled with water. I was breathing hard and getting a hard-on as I continued my peeping. Suddenly she looked in my direction and she reached for the blind. I dropped back down on my cot to appear to be sleeping in case she could see me. But when she touched the blind to adjust its position, it suddenly snapped up to the top with a loud BRRRP! I sat bolt upright with my mouth wide open and my eyes even more so as Cousin Rose let out a yelp as she stood there in the bright window completely exposed. She instantaneously crossed her hands in front of her crotch, and then with a panicked look she crossed her hands over her big breasts and then in total exasperation, abandoned attempts to hide the critical parts of her body she reached up and pulled down the blind. This time she was able to leave it as a complete black out.

Boy is she going to be upset in the morning! What a fantastic looksee I got! Better than I ever hoped for - but I'll probably never get another look. I dreamily laid back down on my cot and paid attention to my hard-on.

At breakfast the next morning, I greeted her, "Hi Ro. You scared the daylights out of me last night with that blind - but I want you to know that you made up for it very nicely, and I forgive you!"

"I bet you do, wiseass! Wipe that grin off your face."

"OK," I said as I sucked in my cheeks.

Chapter 14

Baseball

"I'll bat third in the lineup and Gerry you bat cleanup," Billy said as we prepared for our game with the Dorchester Eagles. The Totes, our club, was headquartered at the Young Men's Hebrew Association in Roxbury, and the Eagles were from the Hecht House on the other side of Franklin Park in Dorchester. They trounced us the last time we played about six months prior. I was pleased to hear Billy's direction since that meant that he, our team captain, acknowledged that I, the youngest kid in the club, was a better hitter than he. He only did this because he wanted us to beat the Eagles this time, and hence he swallowed his pride to present the strongest lineup available. I suppressed my grin and simply said, "Okay."

Because our pitchers were weak our games were usually slugfests, and this one was no exception. In the bottom of the ninth inning with two outs, the score was Eagles fourteen, Totes ten. Three of our batters managed to get on base with two singles and a walk. Then, with the bases loaded, the crowd exploded when Billy came through with a beautiful home run, and the score was tied and no one was on base. Then it was my turn at bat.

"Come on Gerry, you can do it - hit a home run, and then we don't have to go into extra innings," was the cry coming from a half dozen of my teammates and some spectators too. By now, it was late afternoon and everyone wanted to go home.

The first pitch to me was a groover, and I was ready, swung, connected with a sharp crack - and I was running the bases for a home run. I was elated as I ran across home plate to the accompaniment of all the cheers and the back slapping. The Totes were no longer on the bottom of the ladder - we were rescued from ignominy.

However, a greater pleasure came at the next club meeting where a motion was made, seconded, and ratified that I be made the captain of the baseball team. I was elected unanimously, including Billy - which made me a little suspicious. Then I found out that the duties included lots more than just playing the game and my pleasure dissolved into chagrin as I realized that nobody else wanted the job. Besides calling the shots with respect to the strategy of the game, arranging the lineups, and assigning positions, and worrying about the availability and storage of equipment, I also had to call the practice sessions, contact other teams and arrange for games, make phone calls to be sure that all the players remembered when the games were, and I also had to write a blurb each week for the YMHA newsletter. So, in addition to my recognized title of Team Captain, was the unmentioned subtitle of Club Patsy.

I reflected on the irony of the situation, considering that I never managed to raise enough money to even own a baseball glove! And here I was Captain no less! I played third base at that time, and was in the habit of borrowing a glove from one of the players who was not on the field. This worked fine, and I always had a glove to play with, but it was never a glove that was adapted to my hand. It was never MINE. One day after a practice session, I was the last one leaving the ball field in Franklin Park. As I passed a large tree, I noticed a glove on the grass in the shade. As I examined it on my hand, I also looked around and saw that there was no one nearby and I gradually realized that I was now the proud owner of my own baseball glove! I punched my fist several times into the well oiled pocket and grinned all the way home. *Finders keepers-losers weepers! I can live with that,* I thought.

At least I could live with it until I reexamined the glove carefully after dinner. Under that detailed perusal, I discovered the name Art

Rubin under a flap of leather where the thumb joined the palm. I had met Art several times on the ball field at the park and we had had casual conversations at least twice. He seemed to be a nice enough fellow, but certainly he was not one of my gang. I didn't owe him a thing.

If I don't tell him that I found his glove I'll be able to keep it as my own. But that's dishonest - and I'm not dishonest, so how can I do that? I can do it because I'm captain of the baseball team and I need it. But that's no basis to become a liar and a cheat! Why is that lying - I found it honestly - I didn't steal it. It's easy to say that I didn't know whose it was when I found it because the name was so well hidden under the little flap. I don't have to mention it to anyone, and no one will know.

That was how I convinced myself to keep the glove in spite of my reservations. Every once in a while when I met Art in the park, I avoided looking him in the eye. I used it at every practice session and at four games during the following six weeks, and realized that I hated myself for not having given the glove back to Art . In addition to my not being able to look Art in the face whenever I saw him, I also couldn't look at myself in the mirror.

So now you want to give him back his glove - how do you propose to do that without looking like the jerk that you are? Well, I can't go tell him that I found his mit and that now after using it for six weeks and the baseball season is almost over, I want to return it to you. No-o-o that won't work. Suppose I didn't know whose glove I found until today when I examined it closely and found your name in it. No-o-o, you would have examined it when you found it. Why would you have looked again and just now found that little flap?

Circumstances came to my rescue. The next day in the park, who do I see with a brand new glove - Art.

"Hi Art, how ya been?"

"Fine, how 'bout yourself?"

"Ok too. Say that's a fine looking glove you got there."

"It's not mine - I borrowed it from Fred -and I hate it. It's nothing like the one I lost."

"When did you lose it?"

"About six weeks ago."

"No kidding! I found one about then but there's no name in it. If you can convince me it's your, I'll give it back to you."

"My glove has my name in it and it does look like the one you've got there. Let me see it."

With an inaudible sigh of relief I feigned surprise and handed him the glove - and of course he immediately lifted the flap and showed me his name.

"Couldn't have better proof, could I? Keep it."

"Gerry, I owe you one! Thanks for finding it - I really appreciate it. You can't imagine how much I've missed it."

HE was so grateful to me - but I felt that he was doing ME the favor by taking it back! I no longer needed to try to find a devious means to return the glove and I didn't have to berate myself for having kept it as long as I did.

* * *

To return home after a Totes meeting at the YMHA, I had to walk the length of Brookledge Street to Elm Hill Avenue and then down the hill to my home. One night after our monthly meeting, as I was walking along Brookledge I became apprehensive when I realized a black sedan with four men in it was driving alongside me at the same speed as I was walking. It was about eight o'clock in the evening and pitch dark, except for the occasional street light, none of which was near where I was when I noticed the car. My heart pounded in my chest and in my ears as I glanced around to see where I could run and hide. *Damn, there's a four foot block wall on my right. If I jump up on that, then I could run across the lawn towards the back of the house, but there's a chain link fence blocking the access to the back and - - -* before I could finish those thoughts, I heard the doors spring open and two men jumped out and grabbed my arms.

"Hey kid, where do you think you're going? What's your name? Where are you coming from?"

I was so terrified I couldn't answer their questions.

While I stood there quivering, a third guy came out of the car and was patting me down. "Yep, he's got a kit," he said as he felt my back pocket.

"Wha - what have I got?" I managed to say. Then I said, "Who - who are you guys?"

"Shut your mouth!"

I started to gain a little courage as I realized these men were not going to beat me up or rob me, but they were looking for something I knew I didn't have. The third guy was struggling with my tight rear pocket and he finally got my pen and pencil out.

"Naw I was wrong - it's not a jimmy kit, it's a pen and pencil. Where you coming from kid?"

"I was at the "Y" around the corner at Humboldt and Seaver. I'm headed home."

"He ain't what we're looking for. You can go, kid."

"Where can I go?"

"You said you were going home, so go home.'

"What are you guys looking for? Is it safe for me to walk the rest of the way by myself? It's a pretty dark street"

"There've been some break-ins on the street and we're looking for the burglar. But we've been up and down the street several times with no luck, so why don't you get in the car and we'll drive you home."

I looked apprehensive. "It's ok, we're police." He flashed a badge and I got into the car.

Chapter 15

Franklin Field

Franklin Field, one of the smaller Boston parks, was only a few blocks south of Franklin Park and it was frequently where we went for our club activities. It had several baseball diamonds as well as football fields and tennis courts. Besides our baseball and football games scheduled there, sometimes our fights were as well. Our fights were not always scheduled but the most dramatic one was. It was set for Saturday, September 13, 1941 at 11:00 AM. This came about because one of the Irish Catholic kids from South Boston had challenged one of the Jewish kids to a fight, however, it had gotten out of hand and it looked as though it was going to be a massive battle with a cast of hundreds. Both sides were armed with all kinds of weapons ranging from brass knuckles and knives to baseball bats and even some guns.

"Didja hear that Morty Margolis was challenged to a fight by some Irish kid from South Boston?" Zacky said at our monthly meeting at the YMHA.

"Why? What did Morty say that brought that on?" Billy asked.

"Don't know. But I do know that he has an obscene loud mouth - probably called him a fuckin' Mick or something like that in response to an anti-Semitic comment."

"Y'know what else I heard?" Sidney interjected. "I heard that his whole club - y'know Morty's president of the Stallions - his whole club's gonna go with him to make sure that it's a fair fight."

His whole club? Holy mackerel - that will surely bring a reaction from the Southies. This could be a big fight if it goes beyond the two of them. Whadaya mean IF - it's when!

Then as though he was reading my mind, Mel piped up with, "I heard that the Southies are planning on bringing a whole bunch of guys, and they'll all be armed!".

"Damn, has anyone told Morty about that?" Billy asked.

Mel responded with, "Yah, he knows about it - and I understand that he's getting all the clubs at the Y to be there too. And he's also talking to some of his friends at the Hecht House. Should be one helova party!"

On that Saturday morning swarms of teen-age boys with their various weapons were drifting like ants from all directions towards the Field. What we discovered was that the police had also heard about the scheduled fracas and were also moving to the field. By the time the kids arrived for their confrontation, the police had set up barriers and lines of officers surrounding the field preventing any of us from entering. Instead of the bloody battle that surely would have ensued, we all left with only verbal insults thrown at each other by the loudmouths because the Jews and the Irishers never were permitted to get near each other.

I was really scared and only showed up because I didn't want to look like a coward and not stand up to the anti-Semites. My weapon was one of our Totes baseball bats that I was happy to take home unused. I was relieved because I knew that I couldn't use the bat on someone's head because it could kill him. But then, hitting someone elsewhere on the body might not stop him and how would I know that he wouldn't mind killing me?

* * *

In winter the park department flooded the flat lowest part of the field to freeze over for ice skating. I watched the skaters with envy for several years. Then in November of 1938 I learned that Mel wanted to sell his racing tubes because he wanted to buy hockey skates instead.

"Mel, how much do you want for your skates?" I asked.

"Before I tell you, I want you to look them over - they're in great shape and they look almost like new. Come onna my house, it's only a couple blocks."

At his house he handed me the skates, "Be careful now, the blades are sharp." The bottom of the skates looked great, and the blades looked as though they had just been ground.

"How much are you asking?"

"Three bucks."

I turned them over to examine the shoes. The leather was very supple. Then I noticed that one of the eyelets was torn through. I pointed it out to Mel who replied that there were still enough laces to hold them tightly on my foot.

"How about two bucks?" I said.

" Ok, - they're yours."

* * *

The first winter that I had the skates was great - I spent every spare minute at the Field skating. I was adept at roller skating and it only took a few days for my ankles to strengthen to the point that I was also expert on the ice. I was a nut for speed skating and I spent hours racing around the big oval which was approximately the periphery of the frozen area. Every once in a while, someone would organize a whip and I loved to be the last one on it to take advantage of the high speed when the leader "cracked the whip". This "cracking" was accomplished by the leader who was skating backwards and pulling the long chain of attached skaters along in a gently weaving manner. Then suddenly he'd execute a sharp turn to one side or the other as he accelerated pulling the chain along so that when the tail end came to the turning point, the velocity was greatly increased. At the tail end I would let go of the waist of the person in front of me and go zooming off on my own. The biggest problem was to make sure that I didn't collide with other skaters!

When the wind blew, I'd open my jacket and hold the sides out like sails and fly before the wind. When the ice was smooth, I felt as though I was soaring and I reveled with the wind in my face and the warmth I generated by my exertions. When the ice was lumpy, I concentrated on letting my slightly bent knees act as shock absorbers and still enjoyed the speed.

In the springtime, when the ice became soft, I skated nonetheless. I knew that the water at no point was more that four feet deep and near the edges where I usually skated, it was probably less than two feet deep. Therefore I was fearless about having a wave of thin ice moving along in front of me. Despite the stretching of my normal conservatism, I never did go through the ice and managed to end the season gently and happily.

* * *

During spring and summer, Franklin Field was where we played tennis. I never took lessons, and the first time I saw how the game was supposed to be played, was when the famous Don Budge put on a demonstration. I was excited when I hit a ball back to him after he served a fault. Without batting an eye, I told my friends that I had played tennis with Don Budge!

Chapter 16

Learning to Drive

Sidney borrowed his father's new 1940 Plymouth, and we picked up our dates and headed to Norumbega Park for an evening of dancing to the music of Woody Herman's big band. I had been looking forward to this Saturday evening in April,1941 for several weeks. April was supposed to be spring, but it was still cold.

I sat in the back seat with little Betty, and Sid sat behind the wheel with buxom Barbara snuggling close beside him. The front bench seat of that model car was great for snuggling. We called my date little Betty, because she was short, and in our circle of friends we had a taller one. My Betty was only five feet tall, but solidly equipped with feminine attributes. For me, her most pleasing features were a ready warm smile with sparkling white teeth and a lovely athletic figure that I hoped to explore..

After we arrived and the band was playing, I asked Betty "Shall we dance?" as though I knew how. Zacky, another friend in our group of boys, had shown me how to look as though I was jitterbugging without really doing it. I was anxious to try the approach since I knew none of the steps or routines. As we stepped onto the dance floor, I put my right hand on her waist and took her right hand lightly in my left. I stood still, bending my knees slightly moving my body in a little rocking motion with beat. of the music and marking time with my feet in place. Then on one of the heavy beats, I raised my left hand and pushed her to my left to spin. She then went into her routine while I continued to mark time and bob in time with the music. We continued to face each other as she wiggled her bottom and turned us in a complete circle. I was enthralled with Zacky's method because I was doing next to nothing, yet as a couple we appeared to be nominally expert - because Betty was so good! At the end of the set she said, "Gerry where did you learn to dance so well?" I just smiled.

* * *

This was so different from my first dancing experience about a year ago when I was 14. One Saturday afternoon, Billy told me he had a date that evening to go dancing with Sally Landry and he wanted to know if I'd like to go on the double date with her sister Susan.

"Dancing with one of the Landry sisters?" I exclaimed. "You must be kidding - everyone knows that the Landry twins are the best dancers around. "You know I can't dance a step."

"Don't worry, she'll teach you to jitterbug like an expert. Besides, I can't find anyone else on such short notice."

My eyes lit up as I exclaimed "Great! I'm available." The twins, besides being great dancers were also gorgeous and I was excited. I never dreamt of having the courage to ask one of them for a date.

"Relax," Susan was saying, "just get into the feel of the music. No, not like that, like this."

I felt like a *klutz* as I tried to do the step in time with the beat. But I was completely unsuccessful. I was miserable as Susan tried so hard to get me to dance and I continued to move like a stiff robot.

I was relieved when the evening ended with a thank you and a perfunctory good night peck. I had told Susan on the way home that I was sorry that she didn't get even one good dance all evening.

She smiled and replied, "Don't feel bad about that, it didn't bother me."

After we dropped the girls off, Billy told me not to feel bad about spoiling Susan's evening because he had several good dances with her.

"How'd you do that when she was with me all evening?"

"No she wasn't. They took turns with you all night. They look so much alike you couldn't tell the difference."

I laughed and felt just a little bit better about my lousy evening.

* * *

I was smiling happily because it was the first time I felt comfortable on a dance floor - not to mention actually getting a compliment on my dancing. Zacky had also explained to me how to fake it during the slow dances.

"Just walk around slowly in time to the music," he said. "And by the way, keep your right hand on her back as low as you can." Then he winked and continued. "That let's you keep her hips pressed against yours so she can get a good feel for what you've got there. If you are holding her firmly, she can't arch her body away from you. But don't rub too much - you don't want to - to have an accident."

After three fast pieces the band played "I Cried For You," a slow ballad. As we got onto the dance floor, I gently placed my right hand on her lower back and took her right hand and firmly pulled her to me. I was delighted by the way she snuggled up to me tilting her head up to bring her cheek touching mine. The pressure of her breasts against my chest was distinctly noticeable - and I immediately felt an erection developing. She felt it too and momentarily pressed her cheek more firmly against mine. But then she realized the import of what was happening and I sensed her alarm. She suddenly moved her cheek away from mine and she tried to arch her back to bring her hips away from mine. Her wide eyes carried a strong message of - no, let's not do this. I smiled self-consciously and nodded slowly and eased the pressure of my hand on her lower back and our cheeks again came into contact.

At the end of the evening in the parking lot, we froze until we found where Sid's father's car was parked. Betty immediately cuddled up to me in the back seat as Sid maneuvered the car onto the road back to Roxbury. All the way home, Betty and I held hands and kissed. We didn't hold hands as an expression of affection; it was more a matter of protection - for her. She wouldn't let go of my hands because they insisted on trying to feel her breasts or getting under her blouse or into the waist band of her skirt. She was very efficient at handholding so there was very little groping , but it didn't inhibit our kissing.

Every once in a while, I got a glimpse in the rear view mirror of Sid scowling. For a moment, I thought that he didn't approve of what we were doing, but that didn't make sense since I knew he'd be doing the same thing if he were not driving. So I discarded that thought and continued with my futile wrestling in the back seat.

First we dropped Barbara at her house. Sid parked, left the engine and heater running while he went with her to the front door where they kissed. Then he returned to the car and drove us to Betty's house. I walked her to the front door where we kissed once more and she went in. When I returned to the car, I started to get into the front passenger seat, but found Sid sitting there. He looked at me angrily and said, "Factor, you get behind the wheel. You are going to learn how to drive RIGHT NOW!"

"But Sid, I'd love to learn to drive, but it's two o'clock in the morning and we're sleepy. It doesn't make sense to do it now!"

"After you spent the whole time necking in the back seat while I had to drive, - I can't think of any time I'd be more motivated to teach you than RIGHT NOW! Get behind the wheel!"

I slid into the driver's seat. Then Sid spent several minutes explaining about the three forward speeds and the one reverse on the column gear shift and how the clutch and gas pedal worked.

"Whenever you depress the clutch, you let up on the gas, and as you engage the clutch, you press on the gas."

Then he had me practise a few starts and stops until I could do them smoothly. He also had me do some slow turns.

"Now I want you to drive me home. Take the next left and go down Elm Hill Avenue. Leave it in second gear because it's a pretty steep hill and the engine helps with the braking. And don't forget, you NEVER shift gears without depressing the clutch."

"I understand, I understand. You explained the kinds of things that happen if I shift without the clutch. Don't worry, I'm not going to ruin your father's car." I was gaining confidence very quickly.

As we proceeded down Elm Hill Avenue, I saw a block long area of what looked like wet road. There were still remnants of the winter snows piled on the sides of the road and they had apparently melted during the day. The elm trees on both sides of the road stood like spindly unclothed guards with large white boots.

As soon at the front wheels contacted the dark area, we both realized that the melt during the day had frozen and we were on black ice - and the rear of the car started to slide to the right. My heart suddenly was racing and I was breathing fast - I was scared!

"Ohmygod! My Daddy's new car!" Sidney was petrified and couldn't move. I intuitively didn't touch the brakes or gas and steered into the skid as I had once done on a bicycle. We slid for several seconds down the icy section at about a thirty degree angle until once again we were on dry road.

"Gerry - that was fantastic! How did you know what to do? That was wonderful! All I could think of was us ending up wrapped around one of those elm trees - and what the hell was I going to tell my father! Gerry, you're a natural driver. Next time we go out together, you drive and it'll be my turn in the back seat with my date!"

"I think skidding once on a bicycle helped me know what to do. I'll be glad to drive on our next date, but right now, I'm going to drive to my house, not yours, so I won't have to walk home after we get there, OK?"

"OK, you're right, that's where we need to go."

On the way, he explained how I had to obtain a booklet from the Registry of Motor Vehicles and learn the driving rules for the written test, and how he still had to teach me to parallel park and to start, stop and turn around on a hill so that I could get my license. He would ask his father to let me use this car to go for may driving test.

The day finally came for getting my license. I was very confident about my driving because of Sidney's excellent instructions. I had not only driven his father's Plymouth many times but I had also driven the truck that belonged to the company that Sid worked for part time. That driving I did in the heart of downtown Boston; - I had managed it very well. Hence I had no trepidation as we drove to Somerville for my examination and driving test.

"I hope you don't get Mr. Sherman for your examiner. I hear that he is a picky SOB."

So naturally, he was the one I drew. He took me through most of his routine that I accomplished with no difficulty. I was very careful to use the proper hand signals and avoided making another car slow down for me for any reason. Then he took me to a steep hill on a narrow street and told me to turn around. I had practiced this several times and knew how to do it without touching the curbs, because Sid was emphatic that I would fail if I did. However, the very first time I pulled up the hand brake to hold the car while shifting from forward to reverse, I was horrified to feel the sudden release of the tension on the brake handle - the cable had snapped. Normally if the examiner knew that the car did not have a handbrake, the test would automatically be voided. Immediately after I felt the cable let go, I held the car with the foot brake but I continued to hold the parking brake handle as though it was operating properly. Then using heel-toe techniques that Sid had shown me once, and pulling the parking brake handle as though it was working, I was able to turn the car around without touching the curbs or letting Mr. Sherman know of the problem. As a matter of fact, he complimented me on my test when he gave me my temporary license.

Sid suspected that something had gone wrong because he saw how nervous and sweaty I was. After we left the area, I stopped the car and asked him to drive us home. "What's wrong, Gerry?"

"You're not going to believe this, but the hand brake cable broke the first time I pulled it up. I'm a nervous wreck."

"Incredible! I couldn't tell what happened - but I saw that something was funny about the way you did the turn around. Gerry, you did a fabulous job to pull that off without letting Sherman know. Boy! Did you ever earn your license!"

"By the way, Sid, please thank your father for me for letting me use the car, and apologize for me for breaking the brake cable.

Chapter 17

A Memorable Pops Concert

The next time I went out with little Betty, she was snuggling up on my right and I was driving Sid's father's car while he was in back with buxom Barbara. We were on our way to the Esplanade for an Arthur Fiedler Pops concert. But this time instead of watching and listening from our blanket on the lawn in back of all the chairs in front of the Shell, we were going to enjoy it from a launch drifting on the Charles River alongside the Esplanade. I drove past the concert area and pulled into the parking lot where the launch was docked. We paid our two bucks apiece, boarded, and rushed forward to take seats on the right of the front deck. Our friends who had recommended this mode of enjoying the concert had explained to us that the launch would move upstream past the concert area, and then turn around and slowly idle its way downstream with the concert on the right side.

The program was to start at eight o'clock about one half hour after we boarded. The sun was already down and the twilight was deepening and the warmth of the afternoon was giving way to a slight chill. It wasn't really cold, but that did not inhibit me from putting my arm around Betty and moving up closer to her. As the boat moved upstream we could see the crowds of concertgoers milling around on the shore vying for the best spots to put down their blankets.

"We sure did a smart thing taking the boat," Sid commented.

"You're right, this is very pleasant," I added while both girls nodded.

A short time after we had turned around and started to drift downstream, we were treated to the thrilling sound of the Star Spangled Banner and the sight of the crowds rising in its honor. We remained seated at the request of Roger, the pilot's assistant. We settled in to enjoy the music. The launch operator had provided us with concert programs to know what was being played. After the Tritsch Tratsch Polka by Strauss, the William Tell Overture by Rossini and excerpts from Tschaikowski's Nutcracker Suite it was intermission time and also the time for the launch to turn around and go back upstream. The pilot revved up the engine and initiated a sweeping turn to the left. There was no moon and the river was pitch black in stark contrast to the lights of Cambridge and Somerville on the other side of the river and their shimmering reflections in the water. It was a serene view. As we chugged along upstream, we suddenly heard and felt a loud thump, some hollering and some splashing. The engine of the launch was quickly reversed and we more or less came to a stop.

"What the hell did we hit?" Roger shouted as he ran forward with a large flashlight. What we saw in the black water was an overturned rowboat and three young people splashing around trying to find handholds on the smooth bottom.

In the stunned silence the eery scene seemed to be moving to our left. The pilot struggled to bring the launch to the kids in the water. I lost sight of them as the boat turned. I heard a splash as someone dived into the water. Someone commented that he had lifeguard training. Then people were hollering, "Over there to the right." "Why are we moving away from them?" "Damn, damn." the pilot swore as he tried to maneuver the launch.

A moment later I heard a light scratching sound in back of Betty who was on my right by the railing. I jumped up and standing on the seat - Betty had moved over for me - I looked over the side to see a delicate hand reaching out of the water trying to find something to grasp on the hull of the launch. I bent way over the side with my foot hooked over the rail and reached down to grab the hand when my belt was seized and I was vigorously pulled back from the railing.

"Damn it! Leave me alone - I almost had her! I wasn't going to jump!" I was angry. Poor Betty was almost in tears because it was she who had pulled me back and who was now receiving my ill-guided wrath. I looked over the side again and saw nothing and I could sense that the launch was still slowly moving with respect to the accident scene.

"I'm sorry, I thought you were going to jump in and I remember you once said that you were not a strong swimmer," Betty whimpered.

"It's ok," I placated her. "You did the right thing because if I had gotten her hand and tried to pull her up, I would probably have fallen in - and the boat was still moving - and you may have saved - may have saved - my life." My voice faded away to a whisper as I realized the truth of what I was saying. I took her in my arms and held her close. We both wept.

By then a police boat had arrived and I heard the pilot of our launch shouting, "But they had no lights! How the hell could I have known they were out there?"

We didn't hear any of the second half of the concert as we went back to the dock at full speed. It didn't matter because our interest in music was completely replaced by the shock and sadness of the experience. We didn't even take advantage of the offer to get our money back. We drove home in silence.

The next day in the Boston Globe we read about the accident in which four teenagers were on the Charles River in a rowboat with no lights and that they were struck by a sightseeing launch. Only one boy was rescued. Then the news item listed the names of the two drowned girls and the other boy. The River Patrol was still searching for the body of the other boy. As I read those words, I felt like crying again because I almost had the hand of one of the girls and I might have saved her. But I didn't. Then in my mind I visualized myself falling into the water, trying to hold her up while the launch drifted away and then panicking because I couldn't swim with my clothes and shoes on and becoming an additional statistic. I stopped feeling like crying.

This was without doubt the most memorable concert I have ever attended. But it wasn't the music.

Chapter 18

Blackstone Street

One Sunday morning, playing baseball in Franklin Park with our usual bunch of pickup players, I noticed that Andy who usually played very reliably and well, was making one error after another. After the third time he struck out and the game was over, - our team lost- he and I were walking home together in the same direction down Elm Hill Avenue. The street lived up to its name with beautiful rows of elm trees on both sides providing the delightful feeling of walking through a cool, verdant, sun mottled tunnel. But Andy was still sweating and breathing hard.

"Andy, are you feeling ok? Today was not one of your best days."

"You're damn right it isn't one of my good days! I didn't get home last night till three in the morning, and I'm just plain exhausted."

"What the hell were you doing so late?"

"Well I've got this job with a butcher on Blackstone Street and he doesn't let me go home until his store is completely clean and he has his meat ready for Monday, - and that took us until two o'clock in the morning and then it takes me another hour to get home on the street car. Last night I collected my four bucks and told him 'I quit'".

"You made FOUR dollars yesterday?" I exclaimed incredulously. "That's a pile of money. Tell me the guys name and address, I want to go there tomorrow after school and see if he'll hire me - is that ok with you?"

"No problem – go ahead and see if you can get the job. 'Ts ok by me."

* * *

"Mr. Tamkin, my friend Andy told me that he quit his job with you yesterday, and he suggested that maybe you'd hire me to fill the hole that he left."

I was standing on the sawdust covered floor in front of the counter. He, in his full length bloodstained white coverall, was standing behind the counter that ran the length of the narrow shop, about 25 feet. Toward the back of the store there were two little rooms, one was a toilet and the other was a tiny office. The store front on the sidewalk was only about 15 feet wide with about 5 feet taken up by a double door and the remaining 10 feet was open window normally closed by wooden shutters.

"What's your name kid?"

"My name's Gerry Factor."

"How old are you?"

"I'm 16," I lied.

"Gerry, are you lazy like your friend?"

Damn, how can I answer a question like that? Saying yes of course is the wrong answer, and saying no admits that my friend was lazy!

"Mr. Tamkin, I'm a hard worker, and not lazy and I am anxious to make some money. I understand that on the weekends, you start at 5:00 in the morning on Saturday and work through to the morning of Sunday. Is that right?"

"You've got that right. And it's hard work – do you think you can do it?"

"I know I can – I'm strong." I was getting excited because he seemed to have a positive attitude.

"He probably told you that he got paid $4.00 for the Saturday work – and that's right. But, if you show me that you're a hard worker, I'll raise it to $5.00 after a month. If you're good, I'll want you to stay. You can start next Saturday." He paused for a moment to see my smile and a vigorous affirmative nod. "Great!" I said

He continued, "Let me tell you what we do. From 5:00 o'clock till 7:30 we cut steaks, chops and other meats and line them up on these trays. Then we lift and secure the shutters on the sidewalk and we spread these shelves out the window and put out the meat trays. From 7:30 in the morning till about10:30 at night we hawk the meat and sell as much as we can. When a particular cut is nearly gone, we cut some more. After a while you'll learn how to do that too; at first it'll be just me and Yossi who'll do the cutting. Yossi is the full time butcher who works for me already 12 years. When the crowd thins out in the evening, we start preparing our trays for Monday morning, and we keep at it until we are done. Sometimes we get out at 12:30 and sometimes at 2:30.

"Here, write down for me your name, address and phone number." I complied with his request and then left with a cheery, " See you Saturday at 5:00."

On Saturday morning I got up at 3:30 to take the streetcar and the El (Boston's elevated light rail train) to Faneuil Hall station and then walked five minutes to arrive at Blackstone Street at 5:00 o'clock.

Saturday was the very popular Farmers Market day and farmers came from miles around with their horses and produce loaded horses and wagons . They backed the wagons until the rear wheels were against the curb of the sidewalk and the tailgates were let down to horizontal. Between the narrowing by the wagon tailgates, and the shelves from the stores, the space to walk on the sidewalk was reduced to a mere two feet. And of course, the peddlers from the wagons and the stores were in that space in addition to the massive streams of customers who came every week to buy. By 8:00 in the morning the street was solid with horses and wagons on both sides and the sidewalks were solid with people, tailgates, and shelves of meat and produce; - and this teeming mass was accompanied by a prodigious cacophony.

The sounds and smells were incredible! The peddlers were all hollering "Get your sirloin steaks here!" or "Carrots, carrots four cents a bunch!" or "Chuck roasts! Chuck roasts!" and on and on.

Every time a horse shifted his weight, the wagon would move a little with the accompanying rattles, squeals, creaks and groans. And of course not to mention the sounds and aromas arising from the horses occasionally neighing and splattering their urine and feces in the streets. In the middle of Blackstone Street, the horses stood patiently nose-to-nose and the wagons were all so close that there was barely room for a person to squeeze between them. The street and sidewalks were a solid pulsating mass of people, horses, wagons, meat and produce. Toward the end of the day, a sight to behold, was the wagon somewhere in the middle that sold out early and wanted to leave. He was hemmed in on all sides by other wagons and horses so how could he possibly get out? At first I thought that it was impossible, but then I saw how it was done. The farmer went in front of the horse, and took the reins firmly in hand and started pulling the horse sideways. As the horse moved to the side, the next horse was pushed over too which in turn caused the next horse also to move. As each horse moved, the attached wagon first cocked a little, and then moved a bit more to the side. This happened on both sides of the street as the farmer inched his horse and wagon away from the curb, and slowly worked his way down the street to the intersection. As the departing horse and wagon worked its way down the street, the displaced ones immediately moved back behind it, returning to the positions they had before.

* * *

Winter Saturdays on Blackstone Street were brutal. The only redeeming feature was that the smells were reduced, but they were still there. The shop had no heat at all, so we worked in our multiple layers of socks, long johns, sweaters and jackets, gloves, scarves and stocking hats. At lunchtime, I would leave the store and walk a few blocks into the old red brick tenement Italian section of the North End. If I stayed in the shop, I'd be working while eating my lunch. I always found a heated entryway among the buildings to eat in. I tried not to use the same one more than twice to avoid annoying someone who might complain about my being in their hallway. One day I was sitting on the third step inside a heated hallway when the outside door opened and a little bundled up woman, entered.

She froze when she saw me. She stood there staring at me while I held my sandwich looking back. Then she said something that was completely incomprehensible. I shrugged my shoulders in a gesture of no understanding and raised my eyebrows questioningly. Then she started hollering at me in what I erroneously interpreted as an angry manner, waving her arms and pointing at me, at my lunch, at the stairs, and at the door. I nodded to her and packed up my sandwich, put it in my pocket, stood up and moved towards the door. At that moment she began hollering again and grabbed my arm and started to drag me up the stairs. At that point I realized that she wasn't throwing me out but wanted me to eat somewhere else. I heaved a sigh of relief and said, "OK, OK, I'll go with you; you don't have to drag me." Her face lost its serious expression and took on the warm mien of a sympathetic "Jewish Mother" wanting her offspring to eat well. So here was an Italian lady that I was viewing as a Jewish Mother, - one who could not understand a word that I said and vice-versa.

When we got to the top of the second flight, she opened the door to her apartment and we went in. She immediately sat me down at her dining room table and went into the kitchen. She returned almost instantly with a bowl of hot soup and some Italian bread. The soup had to have been simmering on the stove. Then she served me a plate of pot roast with potatoes and vegetables. I gobbled down these delectable plates and thought I was about to finish, when she brought in a plate of cake and a cup of hot chocolate. My three quarters of an hour lunchtime was just about up, but I decided that I would take Tamkin's wrath and enjoy my dessert and this wonderful, warm hospitality. When I finished, I looked at my watch indicating that I had to leave, and this loving little lady gave me a hug and sent me on my way. I hugged her back and thanked her profusely. I ignored Tamkin's comment when I got back, "You're ten minutes late".

* * *

"Hey putz!"

I was looking down at the beef ribs and the work that I was doing of removing the strips of meat between them and throwing them into a large barrel. I thought Tamkin was calling someone outside the store, so I didn't look up. Then he said it louder and I glanced up and saw that he was looking at me. "Oh I didn't know you were talking to me. What?"

"Stop what you're doing for a minute and help me roll this barrel into the refrigerator."

After that was taken care of, I went back to my rib boning as the job was called. A little later I heard again, "Hey putz!" This time I looked up immediately and said, "My name is Gerry, why are you calling me putz? And what does it mean?"

"You don't know what it means?" he exclaimed incredulously.

"That's right, I don't know what that word means."

"Ask you mother tonight when you get home." He gave me another assignment before I could pursue the meaning with him. I vaguely remembered that my mother had once used that word to describe my father.

That night at supper, I witlessly said, " Oh Ma, my boss said I should ask you about the meaning of a Jewish word. He used it to call me, - he said 'Hey putz' when he wanted me. What does that mean?"

My mother sputtered, "You shouldn't let him call you pu--pu-dat!. It's not - not - nice!" I realized that I shouldn't have fallen for Tamkin's bait, but I still didn't know that the word meant, although I could tell that my mother was embarrassed by her color. But I was stupid enough to say, "But what does it mean?"

"It's a man's - it's a man's, - it's a man's - - it's a MAN."

Now it was my turn to blush.

On the next Saturday I told Tamkin, "Don't call me putz any more. I'll not answer if you do."

Chapter 19

Pearl Harbor

Josh and I were walking again on Blue Hill Avenue. It was the 23rd of June, 1941.

"So, Gerry, what do you think about our communists now?"

"I think the same thing I've been thinking for the past two years, except now it is confirmed and I don't have to have doubts or questions. Now I know for sure that they are all strictly repeating the communist party line straight from Moscow. Do you remember how I used to say that I thought the Commies were way off base with their objections to the 'Bundles for Britain' program. My mother used to tell me that we shouldn't support England because the war was a capitalist war and we have to support the workers - the people. And I used to answer her with - but Ma, the Germans are dropping bombs on them. I'm sure that England has workers too! We should send them all the help we can!"

"What do they say now?"

"Before it was capitalist war, and now, overnight, when all of a sudden Hitler invades Russia, it's a peoples war! What a pile of crap! I'm sure glad I didn't buy into that communist propaganda."

"I'll bet they'll now want a 'Bundles for Russia program!'" Josh said.

In October, 1941 the Lend Lease program was established to permit "neutral" United States to send massive materiel support to England, China, and the USSR.

* * *

On Sunday afternoon, December 7, I was lying on the floor in the living room with my eyes closed listening to a concert being broadcast from New York with my stepbrother Larry. Suddenly the music was interrupted by an excited voice, "We interrupt this program for a news flash. Our naval base at Pearl Harbor has been attacked by Japanese aircraft. Many naval ships have been sunk, and we have suffered many casualties. Stand by for more details. We'll pass them on as they come in."

I sat up and looked at Larry who was sitting with his mouth open and his eyes popping.

"Where the hell is Pearl Harbor?"

"It's our naval base near Honolulu. That's Hawaii. Damn, that's terrible! It means that we're at war." His voice was quivering and he looked as though he was about to cry.

"Haven't we been more or less at war with the Germans in Europe?"

"More or less is a lot different from being AT war! The more or less just means that we were sending guns, munitions, tanks and airplanes. Being at war means that we'll be sending our soldiers and sailors to fight against the Japs - and the Germans too because they are allies. That means you and me!"

He still looked like he was going to cry.

"I just turned 16, won't the war be over before I'd have to go into the service?"

"Maybe yes, and - then again, maybe no.

* * *

In September of 1942, two and a half months after I finished high school, I turned 17. By then it was obvious to me that, contrary to my initial thought on December 7, 1941 that I was too young to be concerned with being drafted, I needed to face that issue head on. I had heard that the services had a program that sent higher IQ soldiers and sailors to college to become engineers. After a little research I found out that the Army program was called ASTP, Army Specialized Training Program. It was also designated A12 and the navy equivalent program was called V12. With further inquiry I learned that I needed to be an enlistee to qualify for either one of those programs. I knew I would be called up in the draft as soon as I turned 18; it made perfect sense for me to volunteer.

Which do I prefer, A12 or V12? I asked myself - *Army or Navy? As an engineer in the Navy it would probably be on a ship. That thought plus the fact that I was not a good swimmer and wasn't crazy about the water pushed me to the Army program.*

In February of '43 while filling in the application for the Army Enlisted Reserve Corps I hesitated when I came to the line "religion". I had two choices, none or Jewish. I certainly knew about anti-Semitism but I also knew that atheists also suffered from discrimination. I flipped a coin – and filled in "Jewish". I was comfortable with that, because even though I did not accept Judaism as a religion, I accepted it as my heritage and cultural background.

Chapter 20

War Work

Josh graduated high school in '41 and was enrolled in Boston University studying journalism. He figured that he could complete at least one year before he'd have to go in the military service. During one of our walks on Blue Hill Avenue in May of '42 he suggested I do the same thing.

"Gerry, you'll be graduating next month, and you ought to do what I'm doing. You know, get in a coupla years of college before you have to go in the service, and who knows, the war may be over by then and maybe you'll be able to continue all the way through without interruption."

"Josh, there is only one thing wrong with that idea – and that is that I don't have the money for even one year at college, never mind two and no hope of getting it from my mother or Mr. Samuels either."

"Oh," Josh said.

"I've been thinking of taking a short course at Wentworth Institute on machine shop practice and then get a job that'll let me save enough money to start college. What do you think of that approach?"

"That's a great idea! I noticed in the Globe that there are pages and pages of want ads for machinists. I don't think you can go wrong with that – especially with your capability with mechanical things."

I was pleased with his comment because I had already enrolled.

Two weeks after school was over, I started the hands-on metal working course at Wentworth. There I learned how to operate a lathe, milling machine, shaper, planer, drill press and grinders.

Wentworth also helped in placing students in jobs; I was referred to the Charlestown Navy Yard. There, in mid 1942, they were producing and repairing ships at a frantic pace and they needed a great variety of skills.

The next morning after the course was finished, I left my house early and went by streetcar, train, and bus to Charlestown. At the Navy Yard personnel office I filled in and submitted the application forms and waited to be called. Finally I heard my name.

"At this moment we're full up with machinists, but desperate for ship fitters helpers. How would you like to do your part in the war effort by doing that job which is so much needed?"

"How does the pay rate for a ship fitters helper compare with the rate for an apprentice machinist?" I asked.

"They're both entry level jobs, so the rates are the same."

"What does a ship fitters helper do?

The personnel guy replied sarcastically with, "You may find this surprising, but his job is to help the ship fitter." I restrained myself from exclaiming "No shit!" and instead calmly said, "I guess I should have asked what does a ship fitter do?"

"Well, the ship fitter is the one who assembles the many pieces of the ship. And sometimes he also does bumping which is a bulkhead straightening process." Although I wanted to, I didn't ask him what is a bulkhead.

"OK", I said, "if ship fitters helper is the open job, I'll take it." I would have taken any job they offered – but I didn't want to appear to be too anxious. I could afford to be independent considering that I was all of 16 years old at the time.

The next morning when I reported for work, I was given my time card and shown how to fill it in and how to use the time clock. I was also given a note with the location of ship fitter Henry

Arsenault and was told in which direction to go to find him. He was bumping on the superstructure of Destroyer Escort DE 231 on the left side of Pier 14. I was awestruck at the intensity of the activity and the incredible level of the noise in the yard. Everywhere I looked I saw men and women, moving like insects all over ships and parts of ships. I had to continually avert my eyes from looking at the flickering blue lights of the arc welders. We had been warned at Wentworth not to look at welding arcs to avoid getting what they called a flash. That was a painful condition that felt like your eyes were full of sand. The screaming grinders and the howling ventilator blowers, the ratatat of the chippers and riveters, hissing and spitting of the flame cutters and welders, hammering of the ship fitters and shipwrights intermingled with the voices hollering back and forth created a breath-taking clamor. I was looking forward to contributing to this incredible racket.

It took me about 20 minutes to find the pier and ship my new boss was working on. When I got off the gangway I asked the first person I saw where I could find Arsenault.

"He's aft," was the reply.

"He's WHAT?"

"Aft, aft! Towards the stern." As I approached the stern of the ship I saw a dejected looking man sitting on a box.

"Mr. Arsenault?" I asked.

"Yes, what can I do for you?"

"I'm supposed to be your new helper."

His eyes brightened and he jumped up and started pumping my hand. "Glad to see you! Glad to see you! What's your name?"

"Gerry Factor."

"Gerry, now I'll be able to get some work done. I'm so tired of borrowing Jimmy's helper one hour at a time. Come on, I'll show you all about bumping." Henry took me by the hand and led me into a nearby compartment.

"Here's all our equipment. This is an acetylene torch and here are the bottles of gas that are burned to heat up a spot on the bulkhead red hot. The other one is oxygen. Now watch as I do it." When he pointed at the spot where he was going to put the heat, I learned that the bulkhead was what I would have called a wall. At the spot where he was going to work, the bulkhead had a noticeable bulge out towards us.

"When the steel sheets are welded onto the I-beams, they warp and bulge like this. And that's what keeps us in business all over the ship except on the hull that uses steel of a much heavier gauge."

He opened the valves on the gas bottles and then one of the valves on the torch and we could hear the hiss as the gas poured out. Then immediately he snapped his flint igniter that was hanging from his belt and with a pop the yellow flame sprang into being with a stream of black smoke. He promptly adjusted both valves of the torch until he had the nice blue smokeless flame about one half inch in diameter.

"See how this area of the bulkhead is bowed out towards us? Well I'm going to heat a spot red hot and then we'll pound on it with a flatter and a sledgehammer. That's where you come in, - you'll start out holding the flatter for me. The pounding compresses the hot steel of the red spot. Then we'll cool it with a water spray from this nozzle. You see the one hose delivers compressed air and the other goes into the bucket of water. It's nothing but a huge atomizer. The spray cools the spot and the metal shrinks and pulls the bulkhead straight and smooth if we do it right. The trick is to know where to heat it. It usually takes more than one spot. Here, let me show you how to hold the flatter in place for me to pound on it. Eventually you'll also do the hammering. I'm glad to see that you look like a husky feller." He put down the torch for a moment while he showed me how to hold the flatter. Then he resumed heating the spot until it was a bright cherry color. The flatter had a handle about four feet long that was loosely attached to the neck of the mushroom-like head in the middle of the steel plate which presses on the hot spot.

"Ok, now put on those leather gloves and hold the flatter up against the spot and hold it steady." Which I did. Henry then picked up the 10-pound sledgehammer and hit the flatter about six times. By then I realized that the flatter was heavy and that it would be difficult to hold it much longer than that. The cooling spray put out billows of steam and I could actually see the bulges on the bulkhead pulling straight. That was how this would-be machinist became a bumper. It was hard work but fortunately I was exhilarated by the challenge and by the evidence of my muscles adapting to the requirement. When I first started swinging the hammer I thought I'd never get through the day. It was a good thing that Henry started me off a little at a time. On the day after each increase he asked me how bad did I ache last night? Eventually I reached the level of conditioning that let me swing the hammer all day long with no discomfort or pain.

* * *

The pace at the yard was frantic, marvelous to see, and dangerous. The German submarines were sinking ships on a daily basis; and the major U.S. effort was to build the huge resource for supplying war materiel to Britain when there was a threat of cross-channel attack by the Germans. Ship production was vital for all the theatres of war. The three shifts overlapped to maximize the continuity of the work. That overtime, plus the fact we worked seven days a week gave us some nice paychecks.

The Navy Yard had two parts to it - Charlestown and South Boston. Between the two yards we were told that a ship was launched every single day! Ships were being assembled on the ways and in the dry-docks, as many at a time as would fit. Bits and pieces of ships were being built in every corner of the yards. The docks had hulls being outfitted and finished all along their full lengths, two and three deep. Sometimes to get to a particular hull we had to cross two others. The frantic pace was not without its cost. Safety measures were severely compromised. It was said that our "casualties of war" numbered an average of one person killed every day between the two yards. I almost became that statistic on two occasions.

One day, as we were leaving the yard after our ten hour shift, Henry said, "Tomorrow we move over to hull number 276 on Pier 18. Our first assignment is to bump the outside bulkhead on the port side of compartment 37 – that'll be the first one you'll come to as you go for'd from the gangway." By the time I arrived at compartment 37, Henry had already borrowed another helper and was all set up and ready to work. The three of us set up a very efficient routine. Henry would select the spots and heat them, and George and I alternated between holding the flatter and swinging the sledge, and then one of us would spray while Henry selected and heated the next spot. About mid-morning we were working a spot right next to an I-beam. For this spot, I was holding the flatter and George was swinging. The height of the flatter head was such that when the head of the hammer struck it, there was still one inch of clearance between the surface of the I-beam and the wooden handle of the sledge. All would have been fine except that George missed the flatter head and the wooden handle hit the I-beam and broke. The head of the sledge flew off and hit the bulkhead, bounced back and hit me on the forehead right between the eyes. I slumped to the deck unconscious. When I came to and looked around, I saw that I was alone and wondered where the others had gone. Oh what a headache I had! I put my hand on my forehead and felt an enormous bump, and decided that I had better go to an aid station.

When I stood up, I staggered for a moment then I felt ok and walked towards the gangway. Halfway down the gangway I was pushed to the right side as two guys in white jackets carrying a stretcher rushed past me hollering, "Look out! Let us through, let us through." I watched them go by thinking that someone must have gotten hurt. Then right after them came two more guys in white coats who also shoved me aside with the same admonitions. On the dock, I walked slowly towards the aid station when I heard some more hollering. It was Arsenault's voice. "That's him! Stop! Stop!" I looked around and saw the first two guys who ran up the gangway now running after me and yelling for me to stop. In the background I could see Henry on the gangway pointing at me. Later I learned that Henry and George both had panicked and then ran off the ship to different aid stations both of which dispatched stretcher-bearers to pick me up. The stretcher-bearers caught up with me and practically threw me down on the stretcher and hauled me off to the aid station where an ambulance was waiting and with siren screaming took me to the hospital. I was protesting the whole way that I was ok and didn't need to go to the hospital. But nobody listened. When we arrived at the emergency room I was rushed into x-ray where it was discovered that I did not have a fractured skull and that they saw no evidence of a concussion either. Nevertheless, I had a three-day paid restful vacation as they watched me for symptoms that never developed.

"With a head as hard as yours, you can't be all bad." Henry chided me when I returned to the job."

Although the bumping work didn't require much thinking, I enjoyed it nonetheless. I was proud of being able to swing the ten-pound sledge all day long with no ill effects. It was a nice feeling being in tip-top shape and seventeen years old.

That was the first episode in which I almost became the statistic.

* * *

"Enough bumping for a while, Gerry, now we've got more interesting work to do. See that tanker, the one with the tall round post on the aft deck? That's the Chemung." I nodded.

"Well that is the king post for the on-deck crane which will be used for loading and unloading deck cargo. See the four long triangular wings on the post. We're going to install horizontal brackets between them for additional strength."

"Great," I said, "sounds interesting."

"Let's go to the warehouse and pick up the brackets."

There, Arsenault showed me how to read the blueprint to identify the part numbers that we needed. Then we filled out the paperwork to order them from the clerk. We took one of the flat bed carts that were there for our use and followed the clerk to the location of the brackets; then the three of us loaded them onto the cart. It took both of us to hold the cart on the down slopes, because the brackets were heavy, but it was easy pushing on the level when we got to the docks. A small crane with the help of a rigger who arranged the ropes moved the brackets from the dock and placed them at the base of the king post on the Chemung.

While we worked near the bottom of the post we managed with a small rolling crane, that was called a cherry picker, to raise and hold the brackets while Henry tacked-welded them in place. Sometimes we had to grind the edges or use the flame-cutting torch to trim them to fit. The difficulties associated with holding the brackets in place at the higher levels on the king post resulted in my second life-threatening escapade during my short Navy Yard career. The shipwrights had erected scaffolding and ladders on and around the post for us to install the brackets above the lowest levels, which we had handled with the cherry picker. At the intermediate levels, we muscled the brackets into place with the help of two other men and block and tackle equipment. We were working at the third level, which was next to the top with smaller brackets that weighed a mere 200 pounds. The brackets were waiting for us on the elevated level of the scaffold when we arrived for work that morning.

We ran a rope over the rail of the scaffold about 18 feet above us and Henry and I hauled the bracket up to the required height. We were not comfortable with the process because the ship was in the water alongside the pier. The combined effect of the wind and waves rocked the ship slightly. That was the bad news; but the good news was that the bracket fit without any trimming.

"Gerry, you hold it in place while I get up on the ladder to tack-weld it. Now be sure to hold it steady because it weighs more than you do and if you break the friction of the rope over that rail, it'll come down and you'll go up. Understand?"

"Don't worry," I said, "I've got a good solid grip on this baby!" I checked the wrap of the rope around my right hand.

Henry, holding the welder handle that was already fitted with the appropriate electrode, stepped back up on the ladder that was leaning against the edge of the wing. With the corner of the bracket at the edge of the wing he struck the arc to tack it into place. When he did that, a small spark of molten metal dropped down my back inside my shirt and I flinched sending a wave up the rope. When that wave reached the rail above, the friction was released and the full weight of the bracket broke the miniscule weld that Henry had made and down it went – and up I went! As I went up I tried to visualize what was about to happen when my hand reached the railing above and how I was either going to let go or lose a hand – and either way then fall about 40 feet to the deck below! But luck was with me and the bracket jammed between the two wings, leaving me dangling several feet above the scaffold platform from which I had just been launched.

To say that I was petrified would be a gross understatement. Adding to my petrifaction was the rocking of the ship which was amplified by the height of the king post and the length of the rope from which I was dangling. As I held on for dear life, one moment I was over the dock, then over the deck and then over the water and then deck again and on and on - it seemed like forever. I kept looking down like an icicle frozen solid to that rope. I heard some hollering but couldn't make out what was being said. Finally I felt someone grab my heel and stopped me from swinging. I saw that it was Henry standing on the ladder and he was hollering, "When I tell you to let go, - let go!"

I couldn't say a word because my voice box was included in my solidified state.

"Let go!" he bellowed.

I did nothing. But I was beginning to think just a little and I sensed that he had timed his holler to correspond with what would have been the middle of a swing.

"Look," Henry said sternly, "I've got three other guys here and we've put an extra plank on the scaffold and we're going to catch you and you're not going to bounce off under the rail! So when I holler let go – goddammit – let go! He paused then, "LET GO!"

I couldn't let go. My hand was completely numb.

"Gerry, if that bracket lets go before you do, you'll lose your hand! Now on the next swing you fuckin' well better let go or I'll personally beat your ass when we do get you down – even if you have only one hand! LET GO - - NOW!!"

That little mention of the bracket got my attention. I managed to unwrap my hand from the rope and down I went. There were hands all over me when I collapsed on the boards of the scaffold, and two guys actually jumped on top of me to prevent me from rolling off the edge under the handrail. I lay there for a moment not knowing whether I was going to cry or vomit or what else, I didn't know. Finally I stopped trembling enough to be able to say, "I'm ok now – let me up".

"That was close," one of the men said as he left.

"Let's take a break," Henry said.

"It's ok by me!" I said fervently. Then towards the men as they were leaving, "Hey guys, thanks for your help. I 'preciate it more'n you know."

I rested for about twenty minutes on the scaffold while Henry went down to get another helper. With two of us on the rope and the blood back in my hand, we had no further difficulty installing the brackets.

* * *

The destroyer Kearney had been carefully floated into the dry dock for repair of the gaping hole in its side. It had taken a torpedo and horror stories were being related about the number and condition of the bodies of the sailors being removed from the damaged compartments. The sacks of rotten potatoes that were also found there further aggravated the stench.

I felt the impact of those stories more than I had expected, I guess because I could see the ship and because I visualized the sailors as being just a little bit older than I. And I also thought about their mothers, fathers, wives and girl friends that would be getting the bad news. I almost wept when I thought about that. I was glad I had selected the army instead of the navy.

All those thoughts about the destroyer Kearney came much closer to home when two weeks later Henry said: "Gerry, tomorrow we report to Dry Dock #4, we're installing some interior brackets and baffles in the hold of the Kearney."

When I found Henry on the deck the next morning before we went down into the hold, he took the opportunity to point out some aspects of the planning that went into ship construction and repair in this case. "You'll notice that the deck is in place with that small round hatch open for access," he started to explain. "Before they installed the deck which was also blown up by the torpedo, they put the materials inside for us to assemble--the braces and baffle sections. That violates the normal process, which you'd expect. Usually the hold would be all buttoned up before someone remembered that some big pieces had to go inside – so they could tear it up again, like they do all the time in the Boston streets. You know, first they do the new pavement, and then they get the trenchers to cut it up to put in a new water main or sewer, or electrical cable or whatever! Isn't that the normal way to do it?"

"Yeah, yeah, I've seen it all the time just like you describe it."

"Come on," Henry said with a grin, "Let's go down. Grab those rods and the welder cable and drag it with you, I'll take the grinder and the air hose."

The cable for the interior floodlights was already in place as was the eight-inch blower ventilator pipe. As each new workman climbed down the inside ladder he dragged with him the electrical cable or air hose to power his tools. As Henry and I started to work, I made the mistake of looking up at the hatch through which we had entered. It was full of cables and pipes and it was impossible for anyone to exit through it. I began to suffer my first bout with claustrophobia. I started to sweat even though I was not yet working that hard, and my breath came much faster than usual and I realized that I was trembling. I wanted to scream and get out of there immediately. But I knew that I couldn't get out without causing a huge furor, so I steeled myself to get through this morning and I managed to control my phobia and was more or less effective in following the directions from Henry.

The air blowers were completely inadequate to change the air in the hold anywhere near often enough to provide a reasonable atmosphere to breath. The smoke and other products of the welding, grinding, and flame cutting, accumulated in the hold until we couldn't see from one side to the other. It was difficult to see what we were doing but the worst part of it was the pain in the eyes and the obscured vision both from the tears and the smoke. Considering my claustrophobia and the physical misery from this environment, I resolved, "If I ever got out of this damned hold, I'll never go back in".

At 11:00 the lunch whistle blew and some of the men went up to the hatch pushing their cables and hoses up and someone on the outside pulled them through. Eventually the hatch was sufficiently open and we all went out to eat our brown bag lunches on deck in the open air. I greeted the fresh air and open space with a huge sigh of relief. While we ate our lunch, I said to Henry, " I hate to tell you this ol' buddy but you need to find another helper for the afternoon because I'm not going back down that damned hold. I was claustrophobic down there - I was scared as hell - and allergic too. I had trouble breathing."

"Gerry, that's bullshit – you can't refuse to go back down. The job isn't finished and I need you." Henry was adamant and fatherly.

"That's too bad, but I told you how I feel about it, and I'm just not going to do it. You have to ask the supervisor to find you someone else to help you.

"Don't you realize that if you refuse to do the job assigned to you, that you'll be fired from the Navy Yard with prejudice?" the supervisor intoned with a furrowed brow and very serious face. He wanted to be sure I understood the seriousness of what I was doing.

"What does it mean to be discharged with prejudice," I asked.

"You'll never be able to work for the Navy Yard again."

I raised my eyebrows, cocked my head as I considered what the supervisor had just said for a moment and then asked, "Where do I check out?"

"Same place you checked in."

* * *

That night after I left the Navy Yard with prejudice, I studied the want ads and the next morning I was hired as a machinist at the Star Brass Manufacturing Company in south Boston. Among other things, the company manufactured a testing device for torpedo parts and they also made the parts to be tested.

"Your first job is to trim these weights down to balance against this standard. Let me show you how we do it." The foreman, John, picked up one of the brass disks and mounted it into the three-jaw chuck of the lathe. Then he reached up and slammed the wooden bar to the left actuating the clutch connecting the lathe to the overhead power shafts and the chuck started spinning. With his right hand he showed me how to bring the tool to the work and remove a layer of lead from the center of the weight and then to put it on the balance scale; and then how to repeat the process to sneak up on the proper weight.

I was fascinated by the fact that dozens of lathes and milling machines were all powered by a single large electric motor in one corner of the factory via a network of ceiling mounted shafts and pulleys interconnected by leather belts with other leather belts dropping down to each machine. At each drop, there were different sizes of pulleys on the top and on the machine to permit choices of speeds. Every morning, a long loud screech announced the startup of the motor as the belts slipped on their pulleys, accompanied by a series of slaps until the various belts stabilized. The hum and whirr of the motors and shafts and the frequent belt slaps whenever a clutch was thrown to engage a machine contributed to the total racket of the factory. The clanks of the parts tote bins being dropped at each machine, the chattering of the tool bits on the work, the hollering for more materials, and the blaring radios assured that any occupant of the room had to holler if he wanted to speak with anyone.

"Hey kid, my name's Fred. What's yours?" hollered the fellow in front of the lathe to the left of mine.

"Call me Gerry", I answered. "How long've you been with Star Brass?"

"Three and half years. It's a good company, the owner's a regular guy." Fred had his machine on automatic feed while he took a swig out of a bottle of yellow liquid. He swished it around in his mouth and spit into a wastebasket beside his machine. I deduced that it was a mouthwash. "You met, John, the foreman. He was the one who showed you what to do. He really knows what he's doing; - a nice guy too." He watched his machine while talking with me, and as the end of the automatic cut came up, he skillfully disconnected the feed and retracted the tool, moving quickly to set it up for another cut. While he did that, I was running my machine trimming the weights to the desired values.

Fred was at least 10 years older than I and he seemed very happy to take me under his wing and show me the ropes of the shop and to make sure that I met all the other men. It didn't take long for me to realize that he was completely addicted to the mouthwash, Lavoris. He took a swig about every 10 minutes. He had a case of the stuff in his locker. Some of the men made fun of him because of it, but he just ignored them.

When the weather got hot in June of 1943, I saw that Fred had rammed a long piece of wood into the hole in the headstock of his lathe, and he attached a sheet of cardboard on the protruding end to act as a large cooling fan.

"Gerry, you gotta see this," Fred said as he stood staring into the rotating sheet of cardboard.

"Waddaya see?" I asked while still standing by my lathe.

"You know how the eye can foolya when there's different printing on each side of a spinning thing like this. Come on over here and look."

I cranked the tool post away from the work and walked over to Fred's machine. "I don't see what you're talking about," I said as I peered into the rotating fan.

"Look closer," he said.

As I leaned forward I suddenly felt a deluge of water on my face and I leaped back with an explosive "What the hell is that?" to the accompaniment of a roar of laughter as I realized that everyone was watching me fall for this old gag. Fred stood there with a big grin on his face and the empty jar from which he had just poured the water into the fan to spray the hapless pigeon - me.

"Well thanks anyway for cooling me off." I said sheepishly as I went back to my machine. I should have suspected something like that because this gang was always pulling these gags and pranks. One had to be especially alert to what was happening at your feet, because there was always some clown (usually Lionel or George) giving someone a hotfoot. I thought we were lucky that the place never burned down from those obnoxious matches stuck into the crease between the sole and the upper of the shoe.

"Gerry, I've got to tell you this," Fred whispered conspiratorially. "Lionel and George cooked up the damnedest gag you can imagine for John. You know how every morning he picks up the Globe and how after he finishes it at lunch, he folds it up and sticks it into the pocket of his jacket to take home for his wife to read. When he gets home every afternoon, well, he flips the paper onto the kitchen table for her to read while he goes to take a shower. That's his routine. So, the guys are going to slip a packet of rubbers between the pages of the paper – and guess what – they are going to take one out so there'll only be two instead of three in there. His wife'll go bananas! What a gag!"

"I never met his wife – is she a good sport?" I asked?

"Oh yes – he'll know who did it and he'll explain it to her."

Oh sure! The pranksters wished they had never thought of that gag when it backfired so severely – it almost resulted in their divorce! His wife demanded to know who his girlfriend was and she didn't believe all his excuses. "Those guys work for you – they'd say anything you told them to say just to keep their jobs." That's what we heard was her reply when George and Lionel insisted that it was all their idea. It took their face-to-face meeting with both men in tears before she accepted their explanations and before she forgave John the transgressions that he didn't do. The wise-ass pranksters sure slowed down after that episode.

Chapter 21

Erna

I first met Erna in 1927 when I was only two years old. My parents were living in a three story house on Pilling Street in Haverhill, Massachusetts which was owned by Erna's great aunt. On one occasion her folks were visiting and that's when we first came together. She was also two years old since we were born only 12 days apart in September 1925. Our parents agree that our first encounter was a distinct failure, inasmuch as when Erna mentioned (yes, at two years of age!) that she was going to marry me, I started screaming and toddled away in a panic.

We were 13 years old when we met again. I was walking in Franklin Park with my friend, Billy, who was almost four years older than I. "Take a look at those two good lookers," Billy said poking me with his elbow and nodding his head to the left where Erna was standing with Phyllis. They were intently talking to each other and holding their bicycles. "Let's go talk to them", Billy said. He was about 5' 10" tall, very good looking with dark wavy hair – the girls always seemed to respond very warmly to his pleasant outgoing personality.

"Hi Blondie," Billy addressed Phyllis. Then turning toward Erna he continued with, "My name's Billy, what's yours?"

"Erna."

"Phyllis." She wasn't about to be left out.

I needed only one look at Erna and I was immediately smitten. I loved her dark brown eyes, her dark hair worn in a pageboy style with bangs, her round face and pert little body. I thought she looked terrific in her plaid skirt and pink blouse. I surprised myself when I stepped towards her and said, "What a gorgeous day – isn't it perfect for a bike ride? That's a pretty nice bicycle you have".

"Yes, my grandmother gave it to me on my birthday. I like it a lot."

Billy hid his surprise at my forward approach. While I was physically mature for my age, everyone in the gang knew that I was an absolute neophyte when it came to girls.

How can I keep this conversation going? Damn, she's so cute.

"Have you biked a long way? Are you resting?"

"Not very far, but it's all up hill from my house to here, - so yes, I am resting," she said with a smile.

"I've never owned a bike," I said. "May I borrow your bike for a turn around the field while you're taking it easy?"

"Sure," she said as she leaned the bike over for me to take the handlebars.

"Gee, thanks", I said as I mounted the bike and took off on my ride. I was pleased that she was willing to let me, a complete stranger, ride her new bike. She must be a good judge of character I rationalized. It didn't take long to do the one mile loop around the field in Franklin Park, but when I returned to where Billy and Erna and Phyllis were waiting, I was cursing myself for leaving them alone because Billy was making tracks with Erna while I was gone. As I approached, I heard Billy saying, "Ok, I'll see you tomorrow afternoon at four o'clock at your grandmother's house".

"I'll see you too, tomorrow afternoon," I said, " and thanks a lot for letting me use your bike," as I handed it back to her. "It's a very nice bike," I said inanely.

"You're welcome. See you then."

Then, as Erna and Phyllis rode off, Billy turned to me and said, "She didn't invite you, how come you horned your way in like that?"

"I shouldn't've left you alone with her. I like her and she just might like me better than you, - you never know", I replied. Billy chuckled. As soon as I said those words, I realized how extraordinary they may have seemed to Billy because he was almost 18 years old and considered to be the most successful "ladies man" of our group. I was proud of myself for having spoken up as I did.

"What a cutie! A little young I think, but cute," he said.

"She's not too young for me!" I quickly interjected.

Billy continued as though he had not heard. "I have the address."

I had mixed emotions about these arrangements because I knew that I'd be no match for Billy if he made up his mind to go after a particular girl. On the other hand, Erna did not seem to be impressed with Billy – or for that matter with me either.

* * *

The next afternoon at 4:00 sharp we rang the doorbell at the address Erna had given to Billy. She opened the door and said, "I'm doing my homework but you can come in for a minute if you want."

Wonderful, we've made it to first base! I thought.

She led us immediately into the dining room. An open notebook, several open reference books and a number of papers almost covered the table.

"Have a seat", she said pointing to two chairs on one side of the table, while she went to the chair on the other side.

"This is my grandmother's house, and I often come here to keep her company when she is home – which she is not at this moment, and to do my homework. I have a report to submit tomorrow on the political conditions in England, France, Germany, Spain and Italy, leading up to the first crusade in the 11th century. How much do you guys know about that period?"

"Let me have a look at what you're doing", I said. I hoped that since I was in the 9th grade and she was in the 8th, that maybe I could remember answers to some of the questions she was struggling with. But no such luck.

While I was looking at the history questions Billy was asking Erna, "How would you like to go dancing with me at the YMHA on Saturday?"

"No thanks", came her immediate reply.

I could not dance a step and wanted to ask her instead to go to a movie with me. But before I could find the words I found that she was firmly and unceremoniously ushering the two of us out the front door.

"Sorry fellas, since you can't help me, you'll have to leave. I've got no time for socializing".

"How about tomorrow afternoon?" I asked.

Her reply was a simple, "No".

When we were standing outside on the porch, Billy said sarcastically, "Well, that visit was sure a smashing success wasn't it?"

"Right", I said, " I don't think we were in there a full two minutes. Why d'ya think she was so negative towards us?"

"She was only looking for help with her homework, and I don't think she really noticed us at all." I thought Billy was right. We were both taken aback by her brusque manner towards us. I was depressed for a couple days by what I had interpreted as a very clear rejection. But, being a resilient 13-year-old, I put it behind me – although that pretty face and pert little figure remained in my memory.

During the next four years, I saw Erna perhaps two dozen times in the neighborhood but never had the opportunity – or perhaps the courage – to talk to her. But I still liked her looks.

* * *

During the summer of 1943, my mother and stepfather rented a third floor apartment for the summer vacation season at Winthrop Beach, just north of Boston. Our apartment was one half block from the Crest, the road that ran along the seashore. Even though the beach was very rocky and often beset with icy water and very heavy surf despite the five breakwaters, I enjoyed the family vacations there very much, - especially the active teenage social life. Weather permitting, the days were spent on the beach, where the smooth hand-size gray stones were covered with blankets and mats, which in turn were covered with boys and girls lying beside each other playing the romance and conquest games to see who would end up walking with whom on the Crest in the evening. The parade on the Crest started at about six o'clock and continued to as late as 1:00 or 2:00 in the morning. In the early part of the evening, conviviality abounded and the back and forth banter among the couples and groups was loud and cheerful. After 11:00, the number of walkers fell off rapidly. As the evening wore on, the pairing-off attempts became much more serious and each young man hoped to find a willing partner for some quiet and secluded necking or, if he was lucky some serious petting, or joy of joys, some real sex!

In years past, I had listened to the stories my buddies told of their conquests and I never knew whether to believe them or not – I never had such good luck. I wondered whether they had more on the ball than I did or whether they lied better. Nevertheless, since my friends were all older than I, I listened very carefully to learn about girls and sex.

Within very few days after arriving in Winthrop, I realized that the summer of 1943 was going to be different from the earlier ones because there were very few young men around since most of those over 18 were already in the service. I would reach that age in September. When I arrived early in June, I beamed when I discovered that the girls were running after me instead of vice versa! I immediately started going with Marilyn, the 17-year-old girl who was staying in the second floor apartment of the same building we were staying in. She had a good sense of humor, was an interesting conversationalist, not bad looking and most important, she had a great pair of round tits which I was sure I could eventually get to feel by virtue of the opportunities afforded by living in the same house. I had never felt tits so I had established that as a goal for myself before I got too old. I had no idea as to how old was "too old", however I was confident that I could reach that pinnacle of success by the end of the summer.

One evening, as Marilyn and I descended the stairs of the 1910's Victorian style house to the street for our evening walk on the Crest, I saw three girls approaching from the left. I immediately recognized that one of them was Erna for whom I had kept an eye out during the past four years since I had first met her. I knew she would not remember me.

"Let's walk on Shirley Avenue tonight," Marilyn said as she took my arm and quickly steered me off to the right away from the crest.

"Hi Marilyn!" chorused the three approaching young ladies. "How've you been? We didn't see you on the beach today."

Unsmiling, Marilyn slowed only a little and answered, "I don't know why, I was there," and she kept on walking with a firm hold on my arm. Erna and her two friends however were not to be thwarted in their attempt to meet the new boy they had seen with Marilyn and they were immediately abreast.

"Aren't you going to introduce us Marilyn?"

"Oh, of course, - Erna, Phyllis, and Mim, this is Gerry", Marilyn said reluctantly. She managed to put on a strained smile trying unsuccessfully to appear nonchalant and gracious. Marilyn managed to shake off the other three girls and she and I had a pleasant uneventful walk on Shirley Avenue then back along the crest. I frequently fell back a half step so that I could peer down her ample cleavage. Although I studied and thought a lot about Marilyn's bosom, I found that my thoughts were more often occupied by Erna. Not Erna's bosom, just Erna. Marilyn didn't know it yet, but fatal damage had been done to our budding relationship. Later as I said goodnight to Marilyn, I realized that I had abandoned my plan to give her a goodnight kiss that was going to be more than a peck on the cheek. Originally I had planned on a real passionate kiss and maybe a feel through her clothes, - and who knows what else. I was very aware that here I was at the ripe old age of 17 and my total sex education had been limited to stories from my friends, an occasional glimpse of a "dirty" postcard, and masturbating. I had had some girl friends with whom I had "gone steady" but none of them ever let me feel them or even French kiss them. My friends all talked about their conquests but I hadn't even scratched the surface, never mind caressed it. Not only that, I couldn't discern whether my friends were telling true stories or not – and that frustrated me even more. So while I was saying goodnight to Marilyn, I was formulating my plans for how I was going to get close to Erna the next day.

I was walking the Crest by 9:30 AM to catch Erna and her good-looking friends before they could be found by other young men who had either not yet gone into the service or who were home on leave or furlough. At about 10:15 I spotted the trio strolling towards me with their beach bags and blankets. I stopped, leaned against the pipe railings and waited for them to reach me. Trying hard to appear nonchalant, I immediately accepted their invitation to join them on the beach.

"How was your walk last night?" Erna asked.

"Oh, it was very pleasant," I replied, "The breeze was nice and balmy. We didn't get very personal." I looked into her dark brown eyes hoping that she'd figure out that I'd like to get personal with her. She looked into my eyes too and I sensed that there was some communication – but I didn't know how much. Then I asked, "Do you remember when we met four years ago?"

She looked at me with surprise, "We met before?"

"Yep, in Franklin Park, you let me ride your bike around the field while you spoke with my friend Billy. Then we came to your grandma's house the next afternoon. You were doing your history homework and we couldn't help you, so you threw us out!"

"I barely remember that." Her brow furrowed. Then she laughed and said, "I wouldn't do that now." She blushed when she saw my eyes light up. She hadn't intended to be so forward. Our eyes remained locked together for a moment and I think that was when I fell in love.

"During the past four years, I never forgot you. I used to catch an occasional glimpse of you in the neighborhood but I never got close enough to talk to you. I'm very glad to meet you again."

That sounded inane, but she seemed to be trying to hold back a pleased smile, so I decided to continue in that direction. "I love your bathing suit, it's very attractive or a better way to put it, you look great in it."

She beamed. "I'm glad you like it; it's brand new. It's a Cole". I couldn't care less what the brand name was; my view of her swimsuit was that I liked seeing a lot of her bare unblemished skin. It was a two piece flowered fabric with a small bra-type top which unfortunately did a good job of containing her not very ample breasts. However, with certain movements, I was able to get enough of a peek to verify that she was not wearing any falsies or padding in her swimsuit top. I saw Erna as a beauty. She had a clear complexion, and her dark hair was coiffed neatly on top of her head. Her body was slim and I loved her narrow waist and nicely rounded bottom. I guessed that she was about 5' 4" tall, but I wouldn't give her more than 100 pounds.

I thought that we'd make a handsome couple. I was about two inches taller than she, and I was a bit proud of my stocky muscular build, including a pair of thick, powerful legs. My muscular buttocks made me look a little bottom-heavy in my bathing trunks but not extremely so. Still I was a little self-conscious about that. I weighed 148 pounds at that time.

"Shall we go for a swim?" I suggested.

"You must be kidding! The reason no people are in the water is because it's freezing."

I looked and sure enough, there were no swimmers.

"How about going for a walk?" I said.

"OK."

We put on our sandals and walked along the water edge toward the Highlands. At one point she stumbled on a rock that moved when she stepped on it and I grabbed her hand to steady her. Then I never let go. We were hand-in-hand for the rest of the walk. I loved the feel of her hand in mine and was thrilled when she squeezed back in response to my squeezes.

* * *

That evening, my friend Sidney, who was home on furlough, and I met Erna and Phyllis for the evening teen ritual walk on the Crest. I had assumed I would walk with Erna and that he would walk with Phyllis, so I was taken aback when he said, "Let's flip a coin to see who goes with whom." However, although I hadn't planned on using it, I was prepared for this eventuality.

"OK, I've got a nickel, and if it comes out heads, I'll go with Erna, OK?" I said as I flipped the coin and let it fall to the ground. I stood over it as I told Sid to look and see that it was heads. He looked and nodded his head unhappily because he had hoped to walk with Erna. I picked up the two-headed coin I had carried for years and had hardly ever had a chance to use so effectively.

Our romance blossomed into a wonderful celibate love affair and we pledged ourselves to each other although we decided not to make a formal engagement announcement. During our many hours together we talked about all the subjects that lovers talk about: our likes and dislikes, what schools we attended and wanted to attend, memorable events, religion, sex and marriage. Regarding the last two, there was no question in Erna's mind that they were tightly connected. As far as she was concerned, she was saving sex for her husband.

"But I am going to be your husband. Right?"

"Yes, and when you are, that's when we'll do it", she answered emphatically. "And don't forget, we are only 17 now, and in September you'll be going into the Army, and who knows what - - -." Her voice faded out.

That was a refrain that I heard over and over again. I found her view hard to accept although I knew that it was common. With proper protection I thought that lovers who planned to marry should make love. Erna and I were walking on air during the rest of the summer, - both of us passionately in love. We saw each other almost every day until the day of my induction into the army. During the weekdays I worked at the Star Brass Manufacturing Company; I came home each evening, ate a quick dinner with my family, and then I ran off to walk the crest with Erna.

"I love children," she said one evening, "I want six kids."

"SIX? You're pulling my leg aren't you?"

"No, I'm serious, I really like kids." I noticed that she wasn't smiling.

"Do you have any idea how much money we'll need to raise six children with food, clothes, education and everything else that kids need?"

"I'm not worried," she said, "because I know that you're going to be a successful engineer, and money is not going to be a problem."

I was very pleased with her reply, because I knew that she thought in terms of my desire to become an engineer. "These kinds of decisions can wait till I come back. Let's change the subject and talk about sex instead."

"No, let's talk about what we're going to be doing on Saturday."

"How would you like to go fishing?" I asked.

"That sounds exciting – great!"

On Saturday morning I bought two drop lines with hooks and weights, a can of sea worms for bait, and made arrangements to rent a rowboat. Erna was responsible for bringing the sandwiches and drinks for lunch. At 10:00 we took the rowboat and set out for the fishing area just outside the breakwaters. I was adept at rowing, having learned a lot about it from my experience rowing passengers to the seaplane rides in Revere Beach three years earlier. When we were about one quarter of the way to our destination, I realized that one of the oars was shorter than the other, and I was frequently taking an extra stroke on the left side to keep going straight. If I had noticed that immediately, I would have insisted on a different boat or at least a different set of oars. Later it turned out to be a serious deficit in solving a dangerous situation..

It was a little after high tide when we started out and we had no difficulty in skirting the end of the five breakwaters and moving along the outside of them to the middle of the second breaker. There we found an incredible school of codfish and that was where we stayed for two hours hauling in fish as fast as we could. It was exciting to see the bottom of the rowboat filling up with the flipping fish and anticipating not only some great meals for our families but also some money from selling the rest of them to the fresh fish markets of the area. We had our lunch while hauling in the fish.

Suddenly we were startled by a small wave that splashed over the gunwales of the boat. I looked up and exclaimed, "Damn, look at that sky!" The ominous black clouds extended towards the open ocean as far as we could see and we realized that a squall was coming in very fast and the sea was already covered with whitecaps as the wind picked up.

"We've got to dump these fish or we'll be swamped!" I hollered to Erna above the sound of the wind and the waves breaking on the breakwaters. For several minutes we worked furiously throwing the prized fish overboard. When we had some reasonable freeboard, I grabbed the oars and started to row frantically towards the nearest gap in the breakwaters. The breakwaters were massive elongated deposits of large rocks put there to block the large waves and swells for which the area was noted. The tapered ends of the breakers bounded the 20-foot gaps that were available at high tide. But we had been out there for several hours, and the tide was low so the gap was narrowed to about 10 feet. With the squall there was a substantial swell in addition to the whitecaps. As we approached the gap, I realized that the swell was varying the gap width from about 10 feet at the highest point to about three feet at the trough. When the trough was going through I could see some of the rocks poking up in the middle. I realized that our situation was extremely dangerous. It was going to be tough to time our passage through the gap to coincide with the crest of a swell.

I cursed myself loudly as I realized how negligent I had been for not paying attention to the weather and for accepting a boat with oars of different length. Here I was risking both of our lives for no reason other than ineptitude and stupidity! I was very angry with myself – and scared because I realized that I might not be able to maneuver us through the gap safely. Erna stared at me, terrified, especially since she had never heard me swearing before. Keeping the rowboat more or less centered on the gap was not the major problem. When the swells went through they created a strong current through the gap. Timing was the big challenge. We needed to be close enough to ride the crest of the wave. To see where we were going, I turned the boat around so that we'd go through stern first. The wave carried us forward and it appeared that we were going to pass through ok. Then I realized that we were sliding back into the trough. I frantically rowed backwards not to end up on the submerged rocks in the gap. The different oar lengths caused us to turn. I panicked because the next wave would hit us broadside and we'd capsize! I decided to take advantage of the turning momentum. With several strong strokes of the longer oar I brought the stern around facing the oncoming wall of water. I was terrified as I watched the stern of the rowboat dig into the wave and then pop up with buoyancy that I wasn't sure was there. I felt us riding rapidly on the crest of the wave towards the breakers. I didn't dare look back to see if we were going through the gap or onto the rocks. I tried to gage our situation by looking at Erna's face, but all I saw were two frozen saucer eyes. I used both oars feverishly to keep us aligned perpendicular to the wave. Suddenly the wave subsided and I was looking at the breakers from the sheltered side. We had been safely washed through. As Erna and I both heaved a sigh of relief we heard a tremendous roar above the howling of the wind. She looked up and I turned my head towards the shore and we saw a great crowd of people, two fire engines, and a crew of lifeguards about to launch a lifeboat. The roaring that we heard was cheering because they had been watching our plight and were getting ready to launch a rescue operation. They also were relieved when we washed through the gap. Our friends, fortunately, had known that we were out there and had called for help.

When we beached the boat near the crowd, we were treated like conquering heroes, even though I felt like an incompetent idiot. I did not protest very loudly, and thanked them for being there, especially our friends who had reported our danger – which they had recognized before I did.

* * *

At the end of each evening walk on the Crest, I went with Erna back to the New Winthrop Arms hotel where she and her family were staying for the summer. We lingered on the porch, passionately hugging and kissing, and caressing each other. During these sessions, we had little to say beyond our murmured declarations of how much we loved each other. I often hugged her from behind pressing her strongly against me while I nuzzled and kissed her neck. She had to be able to feel my erection against her backside, but fortunately she didn't wiggle it. I would slide my hands caressingly and gently up and down along her rib cage moving upwards until the underside of her breasts pressed against my thumbs. That was ok – but a fraction of an inch higher, and Erna would take my hand, move it lower and lovingly hold it. Since this tactic didn't work and it was clear that I wasn't going to get to feel her breasts even through her blouse and bra, I switched my attention to her tummy. I was delighted to find that she really enjoyed it when I caressed her abdomen with a gentle circular motion and she permitted me to do that as long as I wanted to. I quickly learned how far down towards her pubis she would let me go before she would take and hold my hand to restrain it from further southward movement. I found that if I extended my little finger, I could feel the roughness under her skirt that was her pubic hair. As unfulfilling as this petting was, I loved doing it because it made me feel so close, so intimate with my sweetheart. I just glowed with love and happiness – in spite of my aching testicles – the so-called blue balls syndrome. I knew that she meant it when she said that she was saving it till we're married – and I had no choice but to accept her decision. Not a single evening with her went by that I didn't rush home to masturbate to relieve my aching genitals. That meant just about every day of the entire summer! I wondered how many of my friends were still virgins at the ripe old age of almost eighteen.

Erna and I were together every available minute of the summer of '43 and the time flew by - weekend days on the beach, every evening together. Our love grew stronger as we knew each other better. Although we knew that I was supposed to go into the ASTP and college, there was always a doubt about the final outcome of the experience, and what kind of a person I would be coming out of the service. So we postponed commitments beyond our unequivocal declarations of mutual love. On my birthday I received the notice to report to Ft Devens for induction into the Army two weeks later.

Chapter 22

Induction
1943

"This is not really goodbye," I said cheerfully, "I'll certainly be at Ft Devens at least two weeks maybe longer, and you'll be able to come visit, and then we can <u>really</u> say goodbye". I was trying to present a cheerful demeanor although I was feeling as though I wanted to cry. Erna and my mother had accompanied me to the train station to see me off and the three of us were standing on the platform beside the car that I was about to board. I reached over and hugged my mother and kissed her and told her,

"Don't worry about me Ma, they are going to send me to college."

"I know dat's vot you told me, but do dey hef to do vot dey say?" she replied.

"They can change their minds, but college is the plan for now, and that's what I'm planning on. If they change the program, they'll probably find some other use for the smart kids they're taking into the service." I said it as though I knew what I was talking about – which unfortunately, I didn't. But it made her feel good, so I said it. As she stood there looking very worried, I turned and took Erna's hands and put them around me as I put mine around her, and we hugged very closely and kissed passionately. My mother's worried look became a broad smile as she saw us embracing. As she got to know Erna, my mother had grown to love her too. I released Erna, grabbed my little satchel and hurriedly boarded the train. I hurried because I didn't want them to see the tears in my eyes as I left. As the train started to move, I looked back and saw that my mother and Erna both were holding handkerchiefs to their eyes too.

At Ft. Devens, I was received along with several dozen other inductees and immediately learned the first basic Army rule "Hurry up and wait!" The non-commissioned officers in charge wasted no time before explaining that "On the double" meant, "run" but at each destination there was invariably a long line to go through. At first the running was not too much of a problem because the inductees were only carrying their little civvy bags, but later as the clothing and supplies were issued, "On the double!" became hell. After filling in the questionnaires and going through the interviews, the entire group of inductees was sworn in together.

In the medical processing line I was apprehensive because I could see ahead along the double line leading to the technician who was giving shots two at a time, one with each hand. Another technician was swabbing bared arms with alcohol while a third tech was handing the shooter two syringes at a time. After I got my shots, I felt a momentary queasiness but felt no other effects. But I was surprised to see that, several of the new soldiers were lying unconscious on cots and that more technicians were ministering to them. Apparently there was no discrimination as to who was permitted to pass out since on the cots were soldiers of all sizes and makes.

Then there was more double time to the supply room for receiving our clothing and other stuff. From that moment on, all pretensions of order were gone because the duffle bags full of gear were very heavy and worse than that, they were very awkward.

Damn, I thought I was in good physical condition. I should be able to carry this bag. But it's too big – where the hell can I grab it? Ugh – those new muscles. I didn't even know I had one there.

By the time the first day was over and we were installed in our barracks and assigned bunks and footlockers, we were all exhausted and sopping wet with perspiration. The next several days were occupied with various tests and classes on the fundamentals of being a soldier. I was worried when I was required to take the Army General Classification Test again because that was the same test I took to establish eligibility for the ASTP. If I didn't do as well as I did last time, or if they changed the threshold criteria, the test results could possibly have a major negative impact on my army assignment to college.

"Hey Sergeant, do I have to take this test again? I took it when I joined the Enlisted Reserve Corps and was assigned to the ASTP."

"Don't worry about it – everyone takes the test."

This reply was not reassuring. I had heard that once you are in the Army, they can do anything they want with you and there is no recourse. I worried for the next several days and then I heaved a sigh of relief when the assignments were formally posted. I was shown going to the Army Specialized Training Program, Basic Training at Fort Benning, Georgia.

Training sessions were held teaching the recruits how to wear and care for their uniforms, basic hygiene, the nomenclature and use of the mess kits, and the main elements of formation and close order drill. We also learned about some of the Articles of War that, among other things, govern behavior in combat. Included in that lecture, was the statement that disobeying orders under fire could result in execution! I knew that this information was superfluous for me because I was going to be in college and not in combat.

"Now one more thing," the instructor continued, "you are to package all your civilian clothing and mail them home or give them to your visitors on Sunday if you have any." As soon as I heard "visitors on Sunday', and as soon as we were dismissed, I dashed to a telephone to call Erna and my mother – in that order.

Despite the many hurry-up-and-wait occasions during the first week in the Army, the time flew by and I found myself on Sunday morning at the Ft Devens railroad station waiting for my two favorite ladies. I saw them alighting two cars to my left. As I moved quickly in that direction, my mother spotted me and with one hand waving, she used the other one to gently shove Erna towards me. I got in several passionate hugs and kisses before my mother arrived to receive hers. *Smart lady! She understands my priorities!* During the afternoon, the level of my mother's understanding was further demonstrated when she announced that she was a little tired and that she would take the 5:00 o'clock train back to Boston and suggested that Erna may want to take the 8:00 o'clock train. Erna and I of course thought that would be fine.

The time till 4:30 whizzed by as I related all the events and impressions of the week.

"Gerreleh, do you hev some new friends?"

"Not yet, Ma, I've been too busy to find time to talk much with the others, and besides, most everyone will be going to different places. I haven't found anyone else yet who is going into the ASTP."

We wandered towards the train station and at 5:00 o'clock I kissed my mother goodbye again. I told her that I would call and let her know if I would still be there next weekend and whether she could visit again. Erna and I held hands and silently walked slowly back towards the central area, each of us momentarily lost in our private thoughts. Then we stopped and turned towards each other and, not caring in the least whether we could be seen, embraced and kissed tenderly. When we separated, I said hoarsely, "Let's find a place where we can be alone". A few minutes later we found a short retaining wall between two small houses in the lodging area of the base. Here we sat and got down to the serious business of heavy kissing and caressing intermingled once again with our breathless declarations of love.

"I'll write every day that I can, even if it's only a postcard," I said.

"I will too," said Erna

Eight o'clock came much too quickly and we were still kissing and touching hands as she boarded the train back to Boston. It was already dark as I watched the caboose receding down the track.

As the week progressed, I was informed that I would "ship out" on Saturday – so I called Erna and my Ma to tell them not to come visit on the weekend and we said our goodbyes on the phone. And then the weekend came and of course, the schedules were changed so I spent a quiet lonesome weekend on base. I played some ping-pong and some pool and I did some reading. On the following Tuesday, though, I packed up my gear and climbed into a railroad car which was headed for Fort Benning. I took my seat and as soon as the train started moving, I found my eyelids drooping and soon I was dozing. As the time passed, I thought about my family and how I had arrived at this present state of being.

I was a very affectionate and demonstrative young man and I had no difficulty in telling Erna, "I love you". My mother had trained me well during the first few years after my father ran out on the family in 1932. My dominant memories of that period are of the smothering love my mother lavished on me. She repeatedly told me how much she loved me, and she insisted that I reply with the same words. I never cease to marvel how I had tolerated my mother's smothering me with love because I realized, even at the tender age of seven that she needed to do that to compensate for the loss of her husband. I shake my head in wonderment at how such a little kid could have been so understanding – and yet, I clearly remember those feelings of that period. But most important to my relationship with Erna, my mother taught me how to say, "I love you" and how to hug and kiss. *Damn, I wish she had taught me how to talk a young lady into the sack!*" And then I laughed as I continued my thoughts with, *No, no, that is not an incestuous thought! I'm not thinking of a demonstration – just some instructions"*. I chuckled myself right out of my doze. I opened my eyes and noticed that the soldier sitting next to me was looking at me strangely. "It's OK," I said, "just a funny dream."

* * *

Despite the dedicated efforts of my mother and my stepfather to inculcate me with the communist way of thinking, I was very much a non-sympathizer with their cause. During 1940 and 1941, I had been unable to understand why there was so much opposition to the U.S. support of England during the early years of the war while the Soviet Union had a treaty with Hitler. The Communist Party line declared that it was an imperialist, capitalistic war and that the "Bundles for Britain" program should be vigorously opposed. Then when Hitler invaded the Soviet Union in June of 1941, the communists declared over night that it was now a "people's war" and that the support for

Britain should be extended to include the USSR. For me that was the crowning evidence of what a fraud the Communist Party line had been in the U.S. They were merely accepting and repeating the line directly from Moscow while attempting to cloak their efforts as being directed towards the benefits of the "working man". In spite of that claim, I had no doubt that the communist members of their upper hierarchy lived much, much better that the ordinary workers.

So here I am now, on my way to Fort Benning, Georgia to help in the war effort in which the USSR and we are on the same side. I don't mind being on the same side with them, as long as I don't have to accept their philosophy that I think is downright contrary to human nature.

Right now, I'm excited about doing my part for the war effort while learning to be an engineer. But first I'll get the infantry basic training at Fort Benning – then I go to college. I am a little concerned, however, because I've heard that Fort Benning is a hard place.

To find out how much of a hard place the Army was for Gerry Factor, read *Private Wars* and learn how the lessons of his childhood helped him cope with his virulently anti-Semitic squad leader and the KKK members in his outfit as well as four Frenchmen who also were intent upon killing him. Not to mention the Germans too.

Private Wars was published by iuniverse.com and can be ordered at any Barnes and Noble book store as well as most other book stores.